# The SQL Guide

## From Fundamentals to Advanced

## Ari Hovi

Technics Publications
SEDONA, ARIZONA

115 Linda Vista
Sedona, AZ 86336 USA

https://www.TechnicsPub.com

Edited by Sadie Hoberman
Cover design by Lorena Molinari
Translated by Lauri Pietarinen and Ari Hovi

First Printing 2025

Copyright © 2025 by Ari Hovi

| ISBN, print ed. | 9781634626705 |
| ISBN, Kindle ed. | 9781634626712 |
| ISBN, PDF ed. | 9781634626866 |

Library of Congress Control Number: 2025931544

# Contents

# Introduction

Welcome to the SQL world!

My first experience with SQL was in the mid-1980s when I was working as a database specialist in a bank's IT department. We got our first PC, equipped with Oracle 4.2, for a trial use. I began exploring SQL queries on the demo database. I had previously worked with traditional Codasyl databases, and I was impressed by how a few lines of SQL could achieve what once took me pages of code. It felt like moving from a shovel to an excavator!

Since then, for the last 35 years, I have taught hundreds of SQL courses, gaining valuable insight into what aspects of SQL are straightforward and which require more explanation. A complete beginner needs different instruction and examples than someone who wants advanced examples. This book includes both. My experience is that anyone can learn SQL!

There have been periods when the media proclaimed SQL obsolete. Yet today, four of the most popular database systems are still SQL-based, and even several top non-relational databases provide SQL interfaces (db-engines.com). At our training and consultancy company, SQL courses, including advanced SQL, are still the most in demand.

In the era of Artificial Intelligence (AI), it may be tempting to rely on AI to generate SQL queries. However, AI-generated queries can still contain errors, making it essential to have a solid understanding of SQL to maintain control. Learning SQL skills is not as difficult as many think, and it is a good investment for the future.

This book contains many examples based on my experience with real projects, helping you get started with SQL quickly and progress to mastering advanced features.

Since SQL dialects vary across database systems, using examples that match your specific product is important. I have tested all SQL statements in this book on Oracle, SQL Server,

DB2, Snowflake, PostgreSQL, MySQL, and Hive. I explain the differences between these systems. Most examples will still work even if your SQL database isn't listed. For instance, the SQL dialect in SQLite, Databricks, Netezza, and Amazon Redshift is similar to PostgreSQL. So following PostgreSQL examples will serve you well.

I thank Lauri Pietarinen for his work in early translation and the many helpful comments.

I'm happy to hear any comments, additions, or suggestions for improvement. Please send them to ari.hovi@arihovi.com.

Good luck on your journey with SQL!

Ari Hovi
Helsinki, Finland

# Ode to SQL

Did you know that the SQL-language is the most commonly used fourth-generation programming language? Java, C, and other programming languages are typically third-generation languages, with a lower abstraction level. In SQL, it is enough to express what you want and the system will automatically figure out how to create this result.

Although SQL is over 40 years old, it is more popular than ever, and there are no alternatives with similar capabilities. New data lakehouse products rely heavily on SQL as well as Snowflake for data warehousing, despite its young age.

SQL has constantly been updated over the years by the ANSI and ISO standardizing bodies as well as database vendors. SQL evolves with time.

Also, most NoSQL databases have a SQL interface. Digging with a Java shovel doesn't make sense when you have a SQL excavator available.

As a result of standardization, many SQL statements work identically across popular products, such as Oracle, SQL Server, PostgreSQL, and MySQL. There are variations, but if you know SQL, you feel comfortable with many products.

SQL also functions as a glue between products, enabling you to choose between hundreds of BI reporting and analytics products for your database. The degrees of freedom are maximized and vendor lock-in is minimized.

SQL can be used in many ways, like interactively or embedding SQL in programs or procedures. SQL statements are often generated by some other product. BI products provide easy-to-use interfaces that automatically translate to SQL and send to the database. Examples include Power BI, Tableau, Cognos, Qlikview, and even Excel.

SQL is well suited for AI tools that also generate SQL. Since these tools are not perfect, it is important to have SQL skills to check the generated code.

SQL is an everyday tool in data warehousing. In the most demanding loading situations, you can use many SQL functions to achieve the best performance—this is called Extract Load Transform (ELT) loading. Popular modern products generate SQL, so good SQL skills are necessary to review them.

Sometimes, it seems like teams avoid using SQL at all costs under the misperception that it is difficult to learn and use. After teaching thousands of individuals, our experience is that everybody learns the basics during a short course.

Many are pleasantly surprised by the power of SQL when moving from simple SELECT * FROM table-type queries to more complex ones. Using the advanced queries presented in this book will save a lot of time and effort in your daily work and take your productivity to a new level.

Learning and deepening your knowledge in SQL is a good investment for the future. It has been one of the most in-demand languages for years. SQL skills will help you remain competitive, and provide you with an edge in AI, data warehouse, data lake, and data lakehouse environments.

# How to Use This Book

The book works well when read from the beginning. It is good to read the section that explains the underlying relational model. SQL commands are introduced from the very beginning, so if you are a beginner, it is worth going in order.

You can easily read selected sections if you are already a more experienced user. To better understand the examples, we recommend having a quick look at the training environment.

You can use this book as a handy reference book. It has a good table of contents and a comprehensive index. Many have left it on their desktop for quick checks.

If you get a wrong result from your query, refer to the list of possible logical errors in this book. Or if you need help with some situation, you will find many useful examples that give you ideas on how to solve your problem.

You can download SQL statements that create the training database for you. You can choose from different versions, including SQL Server, MySQL, Oracle, PostgreSQL, Snowflake, DB2, and Hive. Download the file from https://technicspub.com/sql-guide.

For SQL statement training and exercises, you have three options.

1. **A database system on your computer or at your workplace**. Try to create a new database for training or use an existing database. Download table creation files from https://technicspub.com/sql-guide. Copy the create table and insert statements for your database (e.g., SQL Server) and run them in your SQL interface, and you will be ready to start writing queries.

2. **Use a free online SQL playground**. You can go to one of the URL addresses mentioned below. Copy the create table and insert statements for your database of choice and then write your SQL query. The database is created every time, but

it is very fast, so this is no problem. Use db-fiddle.com. It supports MySQL and PostgreSQL (and SQLite). Download either the MySQL or PostgreSQL create database statements and paste them on the left side. Then, you can write your query on the right side and press Run. You can also save your current view by copying the URL address and opening that URL for the next session. Another free online site is sqlfiddle.com. It supports Oracle, SQL Server, PostgreSQL, and MySQL. Remove the SQL statements that are visible. Copy and paste the create table and insert statements for the database you wish. Write your query after those statements, and end with a semicolon. Maybe it's best then to delete it and write another. Just keep the create table and insert statements at the beginning of the window. A similar tool is db<>fiddle, dbfiddle.uk. There, you can also find DB2.

3. **Download some database software to your computer**. This requires more work, but it is easy to use. You can download SQL Server, Oracle, MySQL, DB2, PostgreSQL, and Hive. For Snowflake, you can create a trial account. After installing the database, download the database creation clauses file from https://technicspub.com/sql-guide. Copy and paste the code and then execute it. Now, your database is permanent, and you can write your queries using the SQL interface available for your product.

There are exercises at the end of the chapters where relevant. You can download the solutions from https://technicspub.com/sql-guide. We recommend that you do not copy and paste examples or solutions but write them yourself. This way, you learn better. After running your query, check that the result set is correct by looking at the tables in Section 4. This is quick because the tables are small.

# CHAPTER ONE

# The Relational Model

All relational databases, including the seven products used in this book, are based on The Relational Model by IBM researcher E. F. Codd, published in 1970. The relational model defines the theoretical foundation of relational databases based on mathematical set theory and predicate logic.

The relational model, as defined by Codd, has become the most used framework for database products. SQL is the standard database language used by almost all database suppliers. Most operational, real-time applications, decision support systems, and data warehouses are based on relational database products. AI systems also use relational databases but often in combination with NoSQL databases and data lakes for unstructured data.

The relational model can be divided into three parts: structure, processing, and integrity rules. Instead of the theoretical side of the model, we briefly present how to implement it in database systems.

## 1.1 Structure

*Table*

The following image shows the departments of a company, and the employees associated with the departments. One department may have many employees, and one employee may belong to one department.

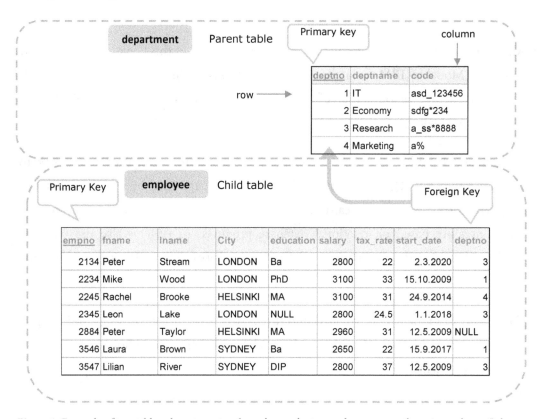

Figure 1: Example of two tables: department and employee. deptno and empno are the primary keys. Column deptno in the table employee points at column deptno in the table department.

Entities such as departments and persons are presented in a relational database as **tables,** such as the tables "department" and "employee" above. A table has **columns,** such as "deptno", "depname" and "code", and **rows**. Sometimes columns are called fields or attributes, and rows are called records. A column has a defined data type, such as numeric or character, and length. All data in a relational database is stored in tables and only in tables.

Tables are set up in the SQL language in its DDL (Data Definition Language) part. For more on this, see Chapter 11, Table Definition and Modification.

### Primary Key and Foreign Key

Each table is identified by a **primary key (PK)**, for example, in Figure 1.1., deptno in the department table and empno in the employee table (both appear underlined). The primary key must be **unique**, meaning that no two (or more) rows in that column can have the same value. For example, each row in the employee table has its own unique identifier. A primary key can consist of more than one column. More on the definition of the primary key in Section 11 on Table Definitions.

Employees belong to departments. A department can have many employees, but one employee may belong to one department only. This is called a **parent-child relationship** or one-to-many relationship. A parent may have many children, but a child can only have one parent, see Figure 2. (In the real world, a child would, of course, have two parents, but in this context, think of one parent, father or mother). To create the relationship, the child (employee) table contains the link field or foreign key deptno that refers to the primary key deptno of the department table. The referencing table is called the child table and the referenced table the parent table. Foreign keys are needed when tables are joined. For more on the definition of foreign keys, see Chapter 11.3. Creating Tables/Referential Integrity.

PARENTS

Department table

CHILDREN

Employee table

Figure 2: Illustration with parents and children. All parents are in one room (table) and all children are in another room (table). Parents have an identification number in the tag (PK). Each child has its own identification number and, in addition, their parent's number as a foreign key (FK) in their tag. They "know" their parent.

## NULL

In Figure 2, Person 2345 has NULL in the column for education. If there is no value for the column at the time of entry, the appropriate value is marked as NULL. It does not denote a blank, space, or zero, but a value that is unknown. The inclusion of NULL implies that relational databases follow so-called ternary predicate logic. When asked whether a certain person has a degree in M.A., the answer will be either true, untrue, or maybe. The result is Maybe if the database entry is NULL. So, there are three values instead of the usual two.

What are NULL values for? Let´s look at a table (see example below) with dates (yyyy-mm-dd), humidity, and other weather measurements. Each morning, new measurements are stored in the table. On the fourth day, December 4, the hygrometer is broken, and humidity is recorded as NULL, an unknown humidity. SQL's function AVG computes average humidity, ignoring NULLs, as it should. If NULLs were not in use, it would be difficult to determine what to record as humidity when the hygrometer is broken. In many contexts, NULL can also cause problems. We will discuss these later.

| date | humidity | Other_measure |
|------|----------|---------------|
| 2023-12-01 | 90 | 35 |
| 2023-12-02 | 87 | 27 |
| 2023-12-03 | 89 | 27 |
| 2023-12-04 | NULL | 29 |
| 2023-12-05 | 87 | 31 |
| ... | ... | ... |

The SQL language has operations for searching NULLs. See the chapter on NULLs. In setting up a table, one can determine whether NULL is permitted for each column.

## Table versus Sheet

Let´s look again at the employee table.

| empno | fname | lname | city | education | salary | tax_rate | start_date | deptno |
|-------|-------|-------|------|-----------|--------|----------|------------|--------|
| 2134 | Peter | Stream | LONDON | Ba | 2800 | 22 | 2020-03-02 | 3 |
| 2234 | Mike | Wood | LONDON | PhD | 3100 | 33 | 2009-10-15 | 1 |
| 2245 | Rachel | Brooke | HELSINKI | MA | 3100 | 31 | 2014-09-24 | 4 |
| 2345 | Leon | Lake | LONDON | NULL | 2800 | 24.5 | 2018-01-01 | 3 |
| 2884 | Peter | Taylor | HELSINKI | MA | 2960 | 31 | 2009-05-12 | NULL |
| 3546 | Laura | Brown | SYDNEY | Ba | 2650 | 22 | 2017-09-15 | 1 |
| 3547 | Lilian | River | SYDNEY | DIP | 2800 | 37 | 2009-05-12 | 3 |

Doesn´t it look like an Excel sheet? Well, there are important differences.

SQL tables are stored in a Database Management System (like Oracle or Snowflake) and they often store huge amounts of rows in a scalable way. Excel sheets are stored in a file and usually are much smaller, but on the other hand, more flexible and visual.

If you open a sheet, it is in memory, and you can easily modify it, many changes at a time. After all modifications, you save the file as a whole (or decide not to save). In SQL, you update rows by SQL statements and the updates go directly to the database (with some tuning possible in transaction management).

In an Excel sheet, you refer to a value by its location, like B5. In a relational table, you refer to data by values. For example, fetch all employees whose salary is 2800.

In relational tables, you can establish relationships with other tables (as described above) to create complex queries involving many tables. This is not the case with sheets.

Spreadsheets are visual and suitable for quick calculations, budgets, etc. But you can easily make typos and mess up your data. Database tables are not that visual and handy, but they are much more reliable in terms of data quality, data security, and performance.

---

## 1.2. Processing

It was Codd's brilliant innovation to base the processing of data on set theory. A table is made up of a set of rows. This set can be subjected to set operations such as "find all employees from London (selection), their first names and last names (projection)". Projection means that we restrict the query to some specific columns, not all columns. Examples of set-theoretical operations that can be performed on a table are given in Figure 3.

Set theoretical operations may be used to process a table or several tables at once. They also apply to updating operations. A single update command, say in the middle of a Java program, may be used to update a large number of rows of a table, without loops. This is high-level programming.

Set theory is implemented by the SQL language, which is based completely on set theory. All the operations in Figure 3 can be performed with different forms of SQL's SELECT statement.

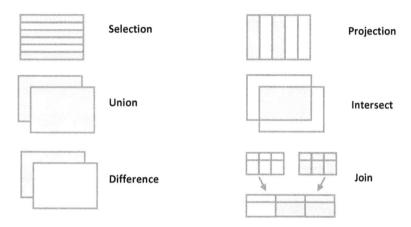

Figure 3: The main set-theoretical operations.

All the columns of a table can be used as search arguments. There is no rule that a column should specifically be defined as a search key.

## 1.3 Integrity Rules

The relational model is also concerned with integrity. A database has **integrity** if its data is correct, consistent, and in accordance with the real world. Integrity is at risk if, for example, an employee is recorded twice, or a person is found to have two towns of residence and it is not known which is correct.

The basic column data types are numeric, string, and date (more on data types in Chapter 11, Table Definitions). The system monitors integrity according to these types. For example, if the data type of the salary column is specified as numeric, you can't insert a row where the salary is a string.

Codd established certain integrity constraints in the relational model. The first is entity integrity. This rule states that the value of the primary key cannot be NULL. In other words, the primary key column must have a value at all times.

For example, you cannot add a new row to the department table without a value in the primary key column. Such a department couldn't have employees in the employee table because there is no parent row primary key to refer to.

| deptno | deptname | code |
|---|---|---|
| 1 | IT | asd_123456 |
| 2 | Economy | sdfg*234 |
| 3 | Research | a_ss*8888 |
| 4 | Marketing | a% |
|  | Administration | ksk |

Figure 4: An impossibility: the row for Administration cannot be added as it has no primary key.

The second integrity constraint is referential integrity. Look at department 1, IT, in Figure 1 (Page 8). It has employees in the table employee. It should not be permissible to remove this department, as these persons would belong in department 1 that no longer exists. In other words, it is not permitted to delete data in the parent table if the child table has rows referring to that parent. Otherwise, persons of that department would be "orphaned" in the department table. This is a loss of referential integrity, to be avoided. Relational database products provide for the control of referential integrity by setting integrity constraints that cannot be bypassed. For examples, see section Referential Integrity.

Of the products discussed in this book, Snowflake and Hive don't support integrity constraints. Their main area is data warehouses, where primary and foreign key integrity is thought to be handled during the Extract, Transform, Load/Extract, Load, Transform (ETL/ELT) process.

## 1.4 Database Design

Proper database design is very important. A poorly designed database is like a house on inferior foundations; there is always something to be fixed. In the case of databases, fixing means unnecessarily complicated SQL programming and loss of data integrity and quality. Database design basically consists of the following steps:

- Conceptual modeling: build a visual Entity-Relationship Diagram (ERD)
- Logical modeling: define tables, relationships, and columns with data types, including Normalization (Normal forms 1NF, 2NF, 3NF, etc.)
- Physical modeling (including specific data types, indexing, and other tuning)
- Create the database with SQL code (written or generated from a tool)

Examples of conceptual and physical models are in Chapter 4.2. We recommend using a data modeling tool.

If you want more detailed information about data modeling, see *Data Modeling Made Simple* by Steve Hoberman.

# CHAPTER TWO

# Properties of Relational Database Products

The following is a brief overview of the properties of a typical Database Management System (DBMS). Though every database provider has implemented the relational model in its own way, the basic structure of the products is surprisingly similar.

## 2.1 Indexes and the Optimizer

In addition to tables, a database has **indexes**. The main purpose of indexes is to speed up searches in the tables. A database index is like a book's index. As the index is ordered, it can be used to look up the desired topic and then jump to the right page without needing to read a book's every page or browse through the whole table. Designing and implementing good indexes requires expertise and is often centralized to database administrators.

Some products don't have indexes. They are mainly used in data warehouse environments. Examples include Snowflake and IBM's Netezza. Their efficiency is based on parallel processing, clever internal partitioning, and other innovations.

The **optimizer** in a database management product is a program that receives a SQL query and tries to find the fastest **access path** for it. The optimizer may decide, for example, whether it is faster to browse through a table or search via an index. More in Chapter 22 on performance considerations.

## 2.2 Data Independence

Better **data independence** is one of the main advantages of relational databases over earlier databases. Data independence makes it easy to establish new tables or add new columns without changing the SQL statements associated with the current database. New indexes can be defined, or old indexes deleted or modified without changing the programs. Changing the row order will not affect the SQL statements, only performance.

A SQL programmer "sees" and processes only tables and columns and gets rows as a result. See the SELECT query in the figure below. He/she does not need to concern himself/herself with the physical aspects of database management such as tablespaces, file storage, or, in principle, even indexes. The optimizer of a Database Management System determines how data is accessed (access path), not the programmer. This is called data independence.

In demanding operational systems, the programmer must nevertheless consider performance considerations and check the sufficiency of indexes for critical SQL statements.

Data independence also implies that row order has no effect on program logic (but may have on performance). As far as SQL statements are concerned, rows are in random order. If you want to output in a certain row order, you must use the ORDER BY clause of SQL.

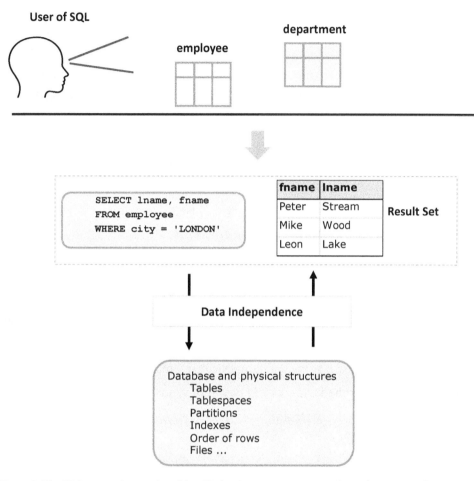

Figure 5: The SQL user only sees the tables. Under the covers are many physical structures that are invisible. Thanks to data independence, the database structure can be changed without changing the queries.

## 2.3 Procedures and Triggers

Stored procedures are program modules stored in the database and launched by the EXECUTE command. SQL is used here, too. Since SQL is a non-procedural language, we also need a procedural language for program logic, variables, loops, if-then structures, and other programming structures.

Unfortunately, such procedural languages differ from product to product. Examples are Transact-SQL in SQL Server, PL/SQL in Oracle, and JavaScript in Snowflake. The procedures can include quite complicated processing rules.

All procedures are in the database, so the network load is light, which gives good performance. Procedure maintenance is centralized. The architecture allows many options for front-end solutions since front-end programs just call the procedures. Front-end interfaces can be changed without changing the procedures.

Triggers are also program modules stored in the database. They differ from procedures in that they are always attached to a given table, and they are started (triggered) automatically by an UPDATE, INSERT, or DELETE command. Triggers are thus not launched by a separate call. Triggers can be used, for example, to keep duplicated data automatically up to date. This is useful because if some data is duplicated – maybe for performance reasons – there is always a risk that the instances will be out of sync. When one instance changes, the trigger fires and updates the other similar instance. Triggers can also be used to perform more complex integrity checks.

---

## 2.4 Views

Views are "virtual tables" set up in a database. Views are like windows into real tables, and they store no data. However, they look like tables and are processed like tables in the SQL language. Set up views with the CREATE VIEW statement.

Views are often used to provide simplified viewpoints to the database, such as to hide complex, multiple table joins, making them look like a simple table.

You can also use views to protect data at the row level. For example, employees in a certain department can be permitted to view rows of their own department only. Views also provide some data independence as many changes can be made to a table without affecting the view. More on views in Chapter 14.

---

## 2.5 System Catalog

Database management systems keep an account of their objects, such as tables, columns, indexes, and users. This data, also called metadata, is stored in the system's own tables (called the system catalog) that can be queried with SQL. There is a table for all table names and other properties, another for column names, etc. More on the system catalog in Chapter 17.

# CHAPTER THREE

# SQL Usage Areas and Background

## 3.1 Components and Types of Usage of SQL

The name SQL comes from the words Structured Query Language. Despite its name, SQL is not merely a query language, but covers the following areas:

- definition and changing of database structure (CREATE, ALTER, DROP)
- queries (SELECT)
- updates or additions, changes, and deletions (INSERT, UPDATE, DELETE)
- control of processing of transactions (COMMIT, ROLLBACK)
- management of authorities and security (GRANT, REVOKE)
- embedded SQL and management of cursors (DECLARE CURSOR, FETCH)
- API interfaces to programming languages.

The part of SQL that deals with the definition and changing of the structure of a database is sometimes called DDL, or Data Definition Language. Queries, updating, insertion, and deletion form the DML part, Data Manipulation Language.

*Databases Understand Only SQL*

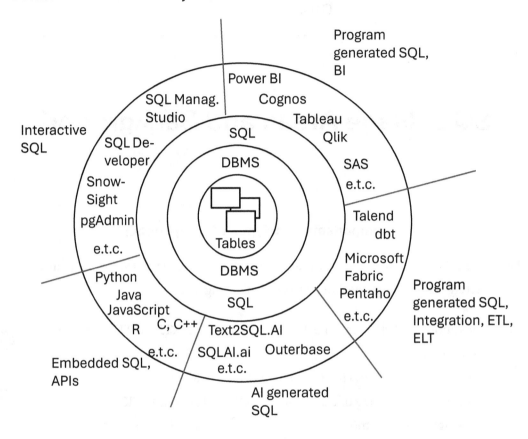

Figure 6: Database Management systems understand only SQL. SQL statements can come from different sources. The products are examples.

In the core of Figure 6 are the tables, where all data resides. The tables are managed by the Database Management System (DBMS) like Oracle, SQL Server, and MySQL. These systems "speak" only the SQL language (except for some database administration functions). So, the DBMS is sitting there waiting for SQL statements to run.

SQL statements can come from various sources. They can be written interactively, using a query interface like SQL Developer (see left upper corner of the picture). Or they can be written by programmers and embedded in programming languages (see left lower corner).

SQL is very well suited as a language that is generated by another program. In the upper right corner, you see examples of BI tools that have a graphical easy-to-use interface. They then generate SQL to communicate with the database. In the lower right corner are data integration tools that also generate a lot of SQL.

The AI revolution leverages SQL, too. In the bottom part of the picture, you see tools that generate SQL, mostly from natural language. Although tools and AI generate SQL language, they do not eliminate the need to know SQL. They might make your life easier, but your effort to learn SQL is worthwhile. In the end, the control of things must be in our hands.

We said that the database only understands SQL. But researchers and data scientists are also interested in other ways to query tables, such as Python. Newer data lakehouse systems like Databricks, Snowflake, and MS Fabric also allow this option.

## Interactive SQL

In interactive SQL, commands are given through a special interface and obtain responses in its own window. Interactive SQL is used a great deal in ad hoc queries, which includes incidental or unforeseen queries. Advanced end users know how to search data for their new needs with SQL, although users have available many other and often more usable tools as well. Programmers may test their queries interactively before embedding them into the programs. They also can examine the optimizer's access path explanations to assess query performance. Database administrators examine the objects and change database structures interactively.

Interfaces to use interactive SQL include:

- **Oracle**: SQL*Plus, SQL Developer
- **SQL Server**: SQL Server Management Studio

- **DB2**: IBM Data Studio, QMF
- **MySQL**: MySQL Workbench, phpMyAdmin
- **PostgreSQL**: pgAdmin
- **Hive**: Beeline, HUE
- **Snowflake**: Snowsight

In addition, third-party programs are available that work with several Database Management systems, such as Toad and DBeaver. SQL Workbench and SQuirreL are examples of open-source products.

## SQL in Programming

SQL statements can also be embedded in a programming language or a report generator. This is called embedded SQL. Here, the responses are moved from the database to variables in the programming language. Statements may be embedded into the program as such, or calls via one of the different API (Application Programming Interface) interfaces may be used to link the program to the relational database. Examples of these are ODBC and JDBC, used by Java programmers.

SQL statements can also be generated dynamically in the program and the generated SQL statement is then sent to the database system for execution (so-called dynamic SQL). Report products and ETL tools often dynamically generate SQL.

SQL is not used to tell how database operations are executed but merely what should be done. SQL is thus a non-procedural language. Typically, a SQL query produces a set of records (rows), while procedural languages manipulate data one record at a time.

SQL also plays a key role in Business Intelligence (BI), where the BI product typically generates SQL statements, which are then sent to a database server for execution. This has made it possible to integrate hundreds of different tools into many different database products. SQL works as a common language ("Lingua Franca" of data management).

In the area of data warehousing, SQL is used for ad hoc and other queries. SQL is also very important in data warehouse loading (ETL/ELT). Modern tools like dbt generate SQL. Every ETL/ELT developer should have good SQL skills.

Often, we need to get data into an Excel spreadsheet from SQL databases. For this, we can use SQL-based MSQuery. Other methods exist, too. SQL acts as the "glue" between numerous end-user devices and SQL databases.

## 3.2 Some History of SQL and SQL Products

In the mid-1970s, IBM was developing a prototype relational database in a project named Project R. SEQUEL, developed by D.D. Chamberlain's research group, was selected as the database language. Later the language came to be called SQL (Structured Query Language).

IBM's first SQL product, SQL/DS, was released in 1981, and DB2 in 1983. The first commercial SQL product, however, was Oracle in 1979. During the 1980s, several SQL-based products were developed, including Sybase, Tandem Nonstop-SQL, Informix, Ingres, and RDB. Later, Oracle bought RDB, CA bought Ingres, and IBM bought Informix.

Microsoft brought its own SQL relational database, SQL Server, to the market in 1989, and the lighter desktop version, Access, was launched in 1991. Open-source code UNIX/LINUX-based SQL databases have become common, the most popular being Finnish-based MySQL, which also comes in a Windows version. PostgreSQL is another popular open-source database. The founders of MySQL created MariaDB, which is compatible with MySQL.

Recently, databases that work only in the cloud have gained popularity, including Snowflake, Microsoft Azure SQL Database, Synapse, Amazon's Redshift, and Databricks.

---

## 3.3 The Standards Situation

An ANSI standard for SQL was published in 1986. Definitions of referential integrity rules were added in 1989. Suppliers began to refer to this standard when presenting the SQL implementation of their product.

In 1992, an important standard version SQL-92 (also known as SQL2) was introduced, with a new noteworthy Join syntax. The new syntax was well received and works almost in the defined form in almost all products mentioned in this book.

The SQL standard of 1999 finally defined triggers and stored procedures, which Oracle and SQL Server had already implemented years ago in their own way. Unfortunately, the standard's new procedural language, SQL/PLM, has not yet become common in products. New object extensions were also included.

ANSI SQL 2003 added more properties relating to objects and data warehousing queries (see SQL and data warehousing below), as well as language elements for interfacing with XML. The latest ANSI Standard is SQL2023.

SQL's programming interface has several parallel standards. Microsoft ODBC has become widely popular, particularly in Windows-based solutions. SQL99 includes a call-level interface for SQL. JDBC has become popular among Java users. The SQL2003 standard defines a new SQL/OLB interface that aims at extending JDBC.

## 3.4 Product-Oriented or Portable SQL?

All the products in this book tend to follow the standard, but there are deviations and proprietary additions.

Differences exist in these areas:

- data types
- functions
- return codes and error messages
- transaction processing
- procedural languages (used in procedures, triggers, and user-defined functions)
- programming and API interfaces

Basic SQL is quite similar in different products, as the examples in this book demonstrate. There are many differences in functions, although some important functions, such as CAST, CASE, and COALESCE (see Chapter 18.1), have become more common. Return codes have also been standardized, but error messages vary greatly among products. There are also differences in transaction processing and concurrence control.

The most significant difference concerns procedural languages used in stored procedures, triggers, and user-defined functions. For example, Oracle has PL/SQL, Microsoft Transact-SQL, and Snowflake JavaScript.

Programming and API interfaces must always be verified case by case. A lot has been done to improve portability in this area, as the examples of ODBC and JDBC interfaces demonstrate.

SQL can be written in many ways depending on the aims. To write as portable code as possible, one should avoid procedures and product-oriented extensions. In this way, it is easy to write an application that works almost the same way in, for example, SQL Server and Oracle environments. This can help the use of the SQL statements of which is as general as possible.

On the other hand, if your company is already committed to a database product and important applications have been made with it, it is sensible to use its handy extensions or procedural languages.

## 3.5 SQL and Reporting Tools

SQL is not a report generator that would format fine-looking outputs. SQL produces a set of rows with a similar structure in raw format that looks like an Excel sheet. In practical reporting, you need intermediate and final totals, special fonts, page numbers, formatting of numerals' decimal parts, etc. These matters are best dealt with by a reporting or BI tool that gets its data via SQL. Thus, SQL can do a complex search in the database's tables with the given search arguments, then the reporting tool formats, computes, and processes the raw data further.

Often reporting systems can also generate SQL code based on users' actions in the graphical user interface or even input of natural language. They are more and more AI-based. Often, you need your SQL skills to check the generated code.

## 3.6 SQL and Data Warehousing

The SQL language has an important role also in data warehousing applications (see Figure 7). Data warehouses are usually SQL-based relational databases and are established because operational systems are often unsuitable for the analysis and reporting of data. For instance, customer data resides in many separate applications and the business wants to get an overall picture of customers.

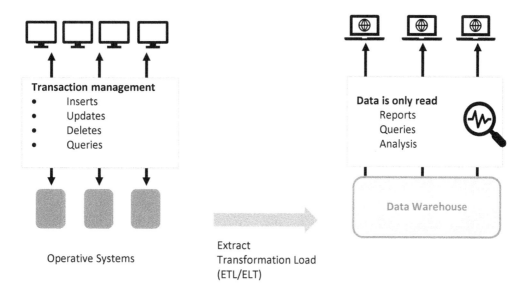

Figure 7: The principle of data warehousing.

Data in different systems are not compatible, recorded history is limited, and system performance is not sufficient for simultaneous analysis and reporting. In addition, data structures are often cumbersome from the viewpoint of reporting and users cannot access data on their own. A separate data warehouse that integrates data can be designed to be easy to use and fast to query.

Development in the data warehouse area has led to data lakes and data lakehouses. Data lakes are used to store large amounts of data, including unstructured data like text and pictures in its original form. Data lakehouses combine the features of data warehouses and data lakes. Both architectures continue to use SQL, at least in the areas that contain structured data.

SQL is used in all the components of the above figure. It is used in the ETL or ELT process to transform and format data for data warehouse structures. Tools like dbt generate SQL for this purpose. Good SQL skills are still a must for ETL developers.

BI tools are used on top of data warehouses for reporting and queries. As described earlier, they also generate SQL.

# CHAPTER FOUR

# Training Environment

Let's introduce the training environment used in this book. The primary key columns of each table are underlined.

## 4.1 Tables

The departments are in the department table. The column deptno is the primary key (underlined). The column code is a secret password.

**department**

| deptno | deptname | code |
|--------|----------|------|
| 1 | IT | asd_123456 |
| 2 | Economy | s''dfg*234 |
| 3 | Research | a_ss*8888 |
| 4 | Marketing | a% |

The table employee contains employees. empno is the primary key.

## employee

| empno | fname | lname | city | education | salary | tax_rate | start_date | deptno |
|-------|-------|-------|------|-----------|--------|----------|------------|--------|
| 2134 | Peter | Stream | LONDON | Ba | 2800 | 22 | 2020-03-02 | 3 |
| 2234 | Mike | Wood | LONDON | PhD | 3100 | 33 | 2009-10-15 | 1 |
| 2245 | Rachel | Brooke | HELSINKI | MA | 3100 | 31 | 2014-09-24 | 4 |
| 2345 | Leon | Lake | LONDON | NULL | 2800 | 24.5 | 2018-01-01 | 3 |
| 2884 | Peter | Taylor | HELSINKI | MA | 2960 | 31 | 2009-05-12 | NULL |
| 3546 | Laura | Brown | SYDNEY | Ba | 2650 | 22 | 2017-09-15 | 1 |
| 3547 | Lilian | River | SYDNEY | DIP | 2800 | 37 | 2009-05-12 | 3 |

According to the SQL standard, the default decimal separator is a dot (.). Local and regional settings may affect its appearance so that it can be shown as a comma (,).

The education of employee 2345 and deptno of employee 2884 is NULL (see the chapter on NULL, Page 62). Your product might show the NULL -values as blank or as a question mark.

We are using the ISO Standard for dates. For example, September 24th in 2014 is formatted 2014-09-24.

The column deptno is a foreign key and it refers to the primary key of the department table.

## project

| projno | project_name | priority | location |
|--------|--------------|----------|----------|
| P1 | BOOKKEEPING | 2 | LONDON |
| P2 | BILLING | 1 | HELSINKI |
| P3 | WAREHOUSING | 3 | HELSINKI |
| P4 | ACCOUNTING | 2 | LONDON |
| P5 | CUSTOMERS | 3 | SINGAPORE |
| P6 | STATISTICS | NULL | NULL |

The primary key of project is projno.

**proj_emp**

| projno | empno | hours_act | hours_est |
|--------|-------|-----------|-----------|
| P1 | 2134 | 300 | 300 |
| P1 | 2234 | 200 | NULL |
| P1 | 2245 | 200 | 300 |
| P1 | 2345 | 100 | 100 |
| P1 | 2884 | 100 | 200 |
| P1 | 3546 | 400 | 500 |
| P1 | 3547 | 300 | 200 |
| P2 | 2134 | 300 | NULL |
| P2 | 2245 | 400 | 500 |
| P3 | 2245 | 900 | 100 |
| P4 | 2884 | 400 | 600 |
| P4 | 2234 | 300 | 400 |
| P4 | 2245 | 200 | 200 |

The table proj_emp ("projects employees") shows which employees belong to which project, how many hours have been used per project, and how many hours have been planned (estimated) per project. Note in particular that each employee can take part in several projects, with differing hours.

The primary key consists of the columns projno and empno together. projno is a foreign key that refers to the project table and empno is a foreign key that refers to the employee table.

All tables have just a few rows. This allows you to easily check the results of your queries against the tables.

## 4.2 Conceptual and Physical Models

The conceptual model in Figure 8, drawn with the data modeling tool Ellie, depicts the structure of the training database. The boxes are entities that represent tables. The "crow's feet" in the diagram shows "one-to-many" relationships between the tables. For instance, for each department, there can be several employees, and for each employee, there can be at most one department.

The small circle in the relationship line means zero, so you can read it like this: "Each employee is associated with either one or no (zero) departments." Peter Taylor is an example of an employee who does not work in any department.

The small horizontal lines are read as "exactly one". For each proj_emp row, there is exactly one row in the employee table and one row in the project table. And indeed, that is the case, which you can easily verify for yourself in the rows of the proj_emp table above.

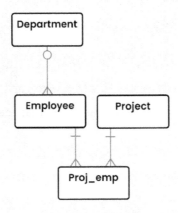

Figure 8: Training database conceptual model.

Below is the physical model, also created using the modeling tool Ellie. Now, we are depicting tables. We can see primary keys (PK) and foreign keys (FK) as well as columns and their datatypes.

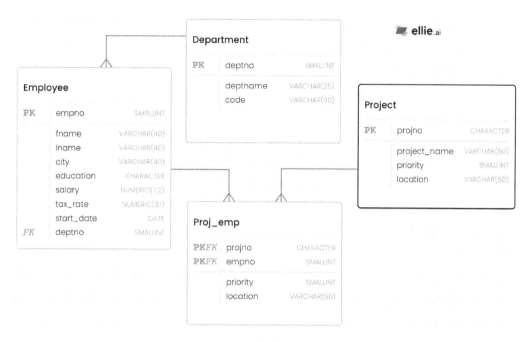

Figure 9: Training database physical model.

After the conceptual model, the logical model (not shown here), and the physical model have been designed, SQL code that creates the tables can be generated using the data modeling tool. This way, database design can be made in a controlled, well-documented way, starting from a conceptual model and ending in generated SQL code that is ready to be passed to the database management system. And your documentation stays in the data modeling tool.

# CHAPTER FIVE

# SQL Background

## 5.1 SQL Databases in Examples

As mentioned in the Introduction, I have tested all of the examples in this book with Oracle, SQL Server, IBM DB2, PostgreSQL, MySQL, Hive, and Snowflake. All statements work with all these databases unless otherwise mentioned. For example, I will mention when a specific SQL statement only works in Oracle.

If your product is not on this list, it is still highly likely that most of the examples will work. For example, the SQL dialect of SQLite, Netezza, Amazon Redshift, and Databricks is quite close to the one in PostgreSQL, which is covered in this book. MariaDB is a MySQL clone, so follow those examples. The examples for Microsoft SQL Server should work in Azure SQL Database, Azure Synapse, Azure SQL Managed Instance, and SQL database in Microsoft Fabric.

## 5.2 Presentation of SQL Statements

In this book, SQL statements appear in separate rows for clarity. However, commands may be given freely. Thus:

```
SELECT empno, lname
FROM employee
```

works exactly the same as

```
SELECT empno, lname FROM employee
```

It is a good idea to write SQL statements in a certain agreed way so that the code written by others is easy to read. This book follows a clear style of writing SQL statements. SELECT, FROM, WHERE, GROUP BY, HAVING, and ORDER BY are on separate rows, as are the AND and OR operators, and the tables of the Join syntax and the ON clause. For the sake of clarity, this book uses uppercase letters for SQL's reserved words (SELECT, FROM, etc.) and lowercase letters for column and table names. However, you can use either uppercase or lowercase SQL keywords and columns.

All products in the book accept that a SQL statement ends with a semicolon (;). However, for the sake of clarity, we do not use semicolons in examples here, unless the SQL statements are consecutive.

---

## 5.3 Comments

A single-line comment starts with two hyphens (MySQL requires a space after the hyphens):

```
-- This is a comment
SELECT empno, lname FROM employee   -- This is a comment too
```

The following syntax can be used for multi-line comments (not in Hive):

```
/* A comment starts with slash-asterisk and ends
   with asterisk-slash and can be multi-line */
```

MySQL also allows commenting by using the hash sign # at the start of the row.

# CHAPTER SIX

# Introduction to Queries

The largest area of SQL consists of queries in different forms. Queries produce a result set, which is a set of rows with the same structure. See Figure 10.

1. A SQL query comes interactively from some source (in Figure 10, it is the interactive query or program) to the Database Management System (DBMS) such as PostgreSQL, Oracle, SQL Server, MySQL, or Snowflake.

2. The DBMS interprets and optimizes the query and makes a physical search operation in the database's tables using an efficient method determined by the optimizer.

3. The rows are returned to the DBMS.

4. A result set is formed with relevant rows.

5. The result set is returned either to the interactive SQL user interface, or to the program to be assigned to variables in the program.

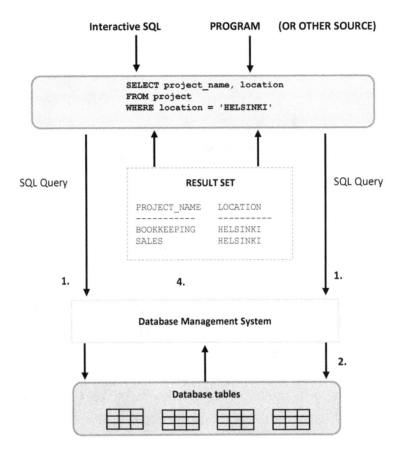

Figure 10: A SQL query and its result set. The source in this picture is an interactive query or program. It can also be a BI tool, AI tool, etc.

## 6.1 Fundamentals

*Structure of the SELECT Statement*

One of the most basic commands of SQL is the query command SELECT. It is made up of the following components:

```
SELECT    which columns are fetched
FROM      from which table/tables/view/views/subquery they are
          fetched
WHERE     which rows are fetched
GROUP BY  how data will be grouped
HAVING    which groups are returned
ORDER BY  how output will be sorted
```

According to the ANSI standard, SELECT and FROM are required and the others are optional. In fact, all products presented in this book except DB2 accept commands with SELECT only (see examples in section Dates). The components must be presented in the order shown above. If ORDER BY is needed, it is always the last one.

The word SELECT is followed by a comma-separated list of the columns we want to retrieve. This is called the SELECT list. The columns in the result set will be presented in the given order, from left to right. A single SELECT statement can contain any column name or names in the tables or views specified in the FROM clause. Using an asterisk (*) will produce a result set that contains all columns of the table/view given in FROM.

*Fetch all rows and columns from the project table.*

```
SELECT *
FROM project
```

| PROJNO | PROJECT_NAME | PRIORITY | LOCATION |
| --- | --- | --- | --- |
| P1 | BOOKKEEPING | 2 | LONDON |
| P2 | BILLING | 1 | HELSINKI |
| P3 | WAREHOUSING | 3 | HELSINKI |
| P4 | ACCOUNTING | 2 | LONDON |
| P5 | CUSTOMERS | 3 | SINGAPORE |
| P6 | STATISTICS | NULL | NULL |

So the asterisk means all the columns of the table. It is handy when you need to quickly see what's in a table. But usually, we do not want to fetch all the columns of the table, just certain columns (see drawbacks of SELECT * in Chapter 10.4 Advice on How to Build a SELECT Statement).

*Fetch project names and locations (see table below)*

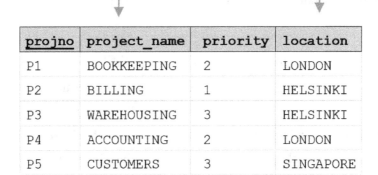

| projno | project_name | priority | location |
|--------|--------------|----------|----------|
| P1 | BOOKKEEPING | 2 | LONDON |
| P2 | BILLING | 1 | HELSINKI |
| P3 | WAREHOUSING | 3 | HELSINKI |
| P4 | ACCOUNTING | 2 | LONDON |
| P5 | CUSTOMERS | 3 | SINGAPORE |
| P6 | STATISTICS | NULL | NULL |

Figure 11: The project table. For this task, only the columns marked with an arrow are retrieved.

```
SELECT project_name, location
FROM project

PROJECT_NAME          LOCATION
----------------      ----------------
BOOKKEEPING           LONDON
BILLING               HELSINKI
WAREHOUSING           HELSINKI
ACCOUNTING            LONDON
CUSTOMERS             SINGAPORE
STATISTICS            NULL
```

You separate the columns with a comma. This is the SELECT list.

*We want to know what different cities exist in the table employee.*

```
SELECT city
FROM employee

CITY
----------
HELSINKI
LONDON
HELSINKI
SYDNEY
SYDNEY
LONDON
LONDON
```

We do not want the same city name repeated in the result. Eliminate double rows with DISTINCT.

```
SELECT DISTINCT city
FROM employee

CITY
----------
HELSINKI
SYDNEY
LONDON
```

DISTINCT suppresses duplicate rows in a multi-column search as well. If the query includes the primary key, DISTINCT is not needed, as primary key values are unique in themselves. Eventual NULL values (see Chapter on NULL, Page 62) are presented in one row when DISTINCT is used.

 **DISTINCT** may slow down processing, so don't use it needlessly. That is because the system may have to sort the rows to remove the duplicates, and sorting might take time.

*Alias Name of a Column*

In the result set, column headings will be the same as column names in the table. Columns may be renamed by an alias name, like alias names lastname and annual_salary in the following query. The alias name will then appear as the new column heading in the result set. In embedded SQL, the program sees the alias name as the column name. Use the word AS.

*Fetch lastname and annual_salary for all employees. The rule is annual salary = 12.5 * salary.*

```
SELECT lname AS lastname,
       salary * 12.5 AS annual_salary
FROM employee
```

```
LASTNAME  ANNUAL_SALARY
--------  -------------
Stream           35000
Wood             38750
Brooke           38750
Lake             35000
Taylor           37000
Brown            33125
River            35000
```

You see here that it is handy to use alias names for calculated columns.

The binding word AS may be left out:

```
SELECT lname lastname, salary * 12.5 annual_pay
FROM employee
```

So, you can use the AS syntax or leave the AS word out. That is, just have a space between the column and alias names. Sometimes, we use the AS syntax and sometimes we leave it out (like in real life).

However, it would be better always to use the AS syntax to avoid the following errors:

```
SELECT project_name location
FROM project

LOCATION
---------------
BOOKKEEPING
BILLING
WAREHOUSING
ACCOUNTING
CUSTOMERS
STATISTICS
```

The intention clearly was to fetch two columns, project_name and location, but as the comma was accidentally left out, "location" was interpreted as an alias name, which then appears as the column heading of project names!

Note: Using SQL reserved words as column alias names in MySQL and Oracle can result in an error message. So avoid aliases like select, from, order, row_number, dense_rank, cast, char, share, and mode. In Chapter 20.12, we will see how to add spaces or other special characters to the column alias name.

## Sorting

We can sort the result set by one or more columns using the ORDER BY clause. Ascending order (ASC) is the default for ORDER BY. If descending order (DESC) is desired, it must be expressly stated. According to ANSI, the column to be sorted must also be included. That is, it must appear in a SELECT list. None of the products in this book demand it, although it is hard to think of a case where the sort column would not be brought to view. Note that without the ORDER BY clause, the row order is arbitrary. One cannot trust that the rows in the table are in any specific order. Row order may be changed for efficiency reasons, and that must not affect the queries.

*Get employee last and first names and salaries in last and first name order.*

```
SELECT lname, fname, salary
FROM employee
ORDER BY lname, fname
```

| LNAME | FNAME | SALARY |
| --- | --- | --- |
| Brooke | Rachel | 3100 |
| Brown | Laura | 2650 |
| Lake | Leon | 2800 |
| River | Lilian | 2800 |
| Stream | Peter | 2800 |
| Taylor | Peter | 2960 |
| Wood | Mike | 3100 |

Ordering by several columns, the second column in descending order:

*Fetch persons sorted by city, within a city, in descending order of salary.*

```
SELECT city, lname, fname, salary
FROM employee
ORDER BY city, salary DESC
```

| CITY | LNAME | FNAME | SALARY |
| --- | --- | --- | --- |
| HELSINKI | Brooke | Rachel | 3100 |
| HELSINKI | Taylor | Peter | 2960 |
| LONDON | Wood | Mike | 3100 |
| LONDON | Stream | Peter | 2800 |
| LONDON | Lake | Leon | 2800 |
| SYDNEY | River | Lilian | 2800 |
| SYDNEY | Brown | Laura | 2650 |

Sorting may also be performed by reference to the sequence numbers of the columns in a SELECT list. Here is the previous query using sequence numbers:

```
SELECT city, lname, fname, salary
FROM employee
ORDER BY 1, 4 DESC
```

We shall return later to using a sequence number in connection with a function, an arithmetic expression, or the UNION operation.

 Although the use of the sequence number seems handy, it is recommended to use an alias name of a column (see below). This way, changing the statement by adding columns to the SELECT list will not mess up the sorting, which can easily happen with sequence numbers.

In the sort, we can use the alias name of a column, such as annual_salary, in this example.

*Fetch city, last name, and annual salary. Use the rule 12.5 \* salary = annual salary.*

```
SELECT city, lname,
    salary * 12.5 AS annual_salary
FROM employee
ORDER BY annual_salary
```

| CITY | LNAME | ANNUAL_SALARY |
| --- | --- | --- |
| SYDNEY | Brown | 33125 |
| LONDON | Stream | 35000 |
| SYDNEY | River | 35000 |
| LONDON | Lake | 35000 |
| HELSINKI | Taylor | 37000 |
| LONDON | Wood | 38750 |
| HELSINKI | Brooke | 38750 |

NULL values (see section NULL Values) come last in Oracle, DB2, and PostgreSQL, and first in SQL Server, Snowflake, Hive, and MySQL. In Oracle, Snowflake, and PostgreSQL, you can change the sorting of NULLS with the keyword NULLS FIRST or NULLS LAST in the ORDER BY clause. The place of Scandinavian characters (å, ä, ö) depends on product settings.

## *String Constant in the Result Set*

You can put a string constant into the SELECT list, and it will appear in every row of the result set. This is actually a new column whose value is the same on each row. You can give it an alias name as you can with other columns. For example:

```
SELECT 'Name is ' AS text1,
        lname,
       'lives in' AS text2,
        city  AS   residence
FROM   employee
```

| TEXT1   | LNAME  | TEXT2    | RESIDENCE |
|---------|--------|----------|-----------|
| Name is | Stream | lives in | LONDON    |
| Name is | Wood   | lives in | LONDON    |
| Name is | Brooke | lives in | HELSINKI  |
| Name is | Lake   | lives in | LONDON    |
| Name is | Taylor | lives in | HELSINKI  |
| Name is | Brown  | lives in | SYDNEY    |
| Name is | River  | lives in | SYDNEY    |

## EXERCISES

1. Select all departments: all rows and columns.

2. Select deptno and deptname from department.

3. In which locations are there projects (fetch from project table)?

4. Fetch the first and last names, cities, and salaries of all employees. Give the 'salary' column the alias name 'monthly_salary'.

5. Order the result of the previous exercise by city and last name.

6. Produce a result set from the table project where the six rows look like these two example rows:

```
text1     project_name   text2           location
-------   ------------   -------------   ----------
project   BOOKKEEPING    is located in   LONDON
project   BILLING        is located in   HELSINKI
```

---

## 6.2 Selecting Rows: The WHERE Clause

Until now, we have selected different columns but have brought up all the rows. We rarely need the whole table, only specific rows. We do this with the WHERE clause, where we can use the logic operators AND, OR, and NOT.

Character string constants are entered in single quotes ('). Character string type data is, for example, CHAR and VARCHAR.

Numerical constants are entered without quotes. Oracle and MySQL do, in fact, accept quotes around numbers as well, but then they cause an additional time-consuming conversion from character to numerical format. In programs where you use embedded SQL, you use host language variables instead of constants.

*Find the first names, surnames and cities of persons from London.*

| empno | fname | lname | city | education | salary | tax_rate | start_date | deptno |
|-------|-------|-------|------|-----------|--------|----------|------------|--------|
| 2134 | Peter | Stream | LONDON | Ba | 2800 | 22 | 2020-03-02 | 3 |
| 2234 | Mike | Wood | LONDON | PhD | 3100 | 33 | 2009-10-15 | 1 |
| 2245 | Rachel | Brooke | HELSINKI | MA | 3100 | 31 | 2014-09-24 | 4 |
| 2345 | Leon | Lake | LONDON | NULL | 2800 | 24.5 | 2018-01-01 | 3 |
| 2884 | Peter | Taylor | HELSINKI | MA | 2960 | 31 | 2009-05-12 | NULL |
| 3546 | Laura | Brown | SYDNEY | Ba | 2650 | 22 | 2017-09-15 | 1 |
| 3547 | Lilian | River | SYDNEY | DIP | 2800 | 37 | 2009-05-12 | 3 |

In the above table, for people who live in London (bold rows), columns lname, fname, and city are selected.

```
SELECT fname, lname, city
FROM employee
WHERE city = 'LONDON'

FNAME        LNAME     CITY
----------   -------   ----------
Peter        Stream    LONDON
Mike         Wood      LONDON
Leon         Lake      LONDON
```

The search condition does not have to appear in the SELECT list:

```
SELECT fname, lname
FROM employee
WHERE city = 'LONDON'

FNAME      LNAME
-------    ----------
Peter      Stream
Mike       Wood
Leon       Lake
```

Pay attention to small and capital letters. Oracle, Snowflake, PostgreSQL, Hive, and DB2 require that the character string is presented in the exact case. Thus, the search condition:

```
WHERE sname = 'Rivers'
```

is different from

```
WHERE sname = 'RIVERS'
```

On the other hand, SQL Server and MySQL will bring the same result set with both search conditions. Do check the situation with your product. If big case and small case characters cause problems, see functions UPPER and LOWER.

SQL's comparison operators are, according to the ANSI standard:

= equals

< smaller than

> greater than

<> unequal, different from

<= smaller than or equal to

>= greater than or equal to

Inequality can also be expressed !=

*Find the persons whose salary is higher than 2800, sorted in alphabetic order.*

```
SELECT lname, salary
FROM employee
WHERE salary > 2800
ORDER BY lname

LNAME     SALARY
-------   ---------
Brooke    3100
Taylor    2960
Wood      3100
```

## AND and OR

The AND operator combines two or more search conditions.

*Find people from London who get paid 2800. In other words, find those whose city is London and salary equals 2800. Get their surname, city, and salary. (See bold rows below)*

| empno | fname | lname | city | education | salary | tax rate | start date | deptno |
|-------|-------|-------|------|-----------|--------|----------|------------|--------|
| 2134 | Peter | Stream | LONDON | Ba | 2800 | 22 | 2020-03-02 | 3 |
| 2234 | Mike | Wood | LONDON | PhD | 3100 | 33 | 2009-10-15 | 1 |
| 2245 | Rachel | Brooke | HELSINKI | MA | 3100 | 31 | 2014-09-24 | 4 |
| 2345 | Leon | Lake | LONDON | NULL | 2800 | 24.5 | 2018-01-01 | 3 |
| 2884 | Peter | Taylor | HELSINKI | MA | 2960 | 31 | 2009-05-12 | NULL |
| 3546 | Laura | Brown | SYDNEY | Ba | 2650 | 22 | 2017-09-15 | 1 |
| 3547 | Lilian | River | SYDNEY | DIP | 2800 | 37 | 2009-05-12 | 3 |

```
SELECT lname, city, salary
FROM employee
WHERE city = 'LONDON'
AND salary = 2800
```

```
LNAME      CITY       SALARY
-------    -------    -------
Stream     LONDON     2800
Lake       LONDON     2800
```

Let's then look at a more complicated example.

*Find all employees from London and employees whose salary is 2800.*

NOTE: The word "and" is here to be interpreted as an OR condition (OR). In other words:

*Find all employees whose city is London or whose salary is 2800.*

| empno | fname | lname | city | education | salary | tax rate | start date | deptno |
|-------|-------|-------|------|-----------|--------|----------|------------|--------|
| 2134 | Peter | Stream | LONDON | Ba | 2800 | 22 | 2020-03-02 | 3 |
| 2234 | Mike | Wood | LONDON | PhD | 3100 | 33 | 2009-10-15 | 1 |
| 2245 | Rachel | Brooke | HELSINKI | MA | 3100 | 31 | 2014-09-24 | 4 |
| 2345 | Leon | Lake | LONDON | NULL | 2800 | 24.5 | 2018-01-01 | 3 |
| 2884 | Peter | Taylor | HELSINKI | MA | 2960 | 31 | 2009-05-12 | NULL |
| 3546 | Laura | Brown | SYDNEY | Ba | 2650 | 22 | 2017-09-15 | 1 |
| 3547 | Lilian | River | SYDNEY | DIP | 2800 | 37 | 2009-05-12 | 3 |

```
SELECT lname, city, salary
FROM employee
WHERE city = 'LONDON'
OR salary = 2800


LNAME      CITY         SALARY
-------    ----------   ----------
Stream     LONDON       2800
Wood       LONDON       3100
Lake       LONDON       2800
River      SYDNEY       2800
```

Thus, it is enough if one of the conditions is satisfied. Some might think of using the following formulation:

```
WHERE salary = 2800 OR 3100     -- This is wrong!
```

This, however, is wrong. The following is correct (we will discuss IN on Page 61):

```
WHERE salary = 2800 OR salary = 3100
```

## The NOT condition

NOT always precedes the entire expression.

*Find employees whose salary is 2800 and who do not live in London.*

```
SELECT fname, lname, city, salary
FROM employee
WHERE salary = 2800
AND NOT city = 'LONDON'


FNAME      LNAME        CITY         SALARY
--------   ---------    ----------   ----------
Lilian     River        SYDNEY       2800
```

The intuitively obvious form AND city NOT = 'LONDON' is wrong.

Perhaps the most convenient way is to use the unequal sign (<>):

```
AND city <> 'LONDON'
```

or the following:

```
AND city != 'LONDON'
```

Note that NULL values do not get selected in a NOT-type search. For a further discussion of this, see the section on NULL values.

## *Parentheses*

Use parentheses if you are unsure of the order in which the logical operators are evaluated. The following example is incorrect!

*We are looking at employees from London only. Fetch the London employees that either have a salary of 2800 or have the degree Ba. We want the fname, lname, city, education, and salary columns.*

| empno | fname | lname | city | education | salary | tax_rate | start_date | deptno |
|-------|-------|-------|------|-----------|--------|----------|------------|--------|
| 2134 | Peter | Stream | LONDON | Ba | 2800 | 22 | 2020-03-02 | 3 |
| 2234 | Mike | Wood | LONDON | PhD | 3100 | 33 | 2009-10-15 | 1 |
| 2245 | Rachel | Brooke | HELSINKI | MA | 3100 | 31 | 2014-09-24 | 4 |
| 2345 | Leon | Lake | LONDON | NULL | 2800 | 24.5 | 2018-01-01 | 3 |
| 2884 | Peter | Taylor | HELSINKI | MA | 2960 | 31 | 2009-05-12 | NULL |
| 3546 | Laura | Brown | SYDNEY | Ba | 2650 | 22 | 2017-09-15 | 1 |
| 3547 | Lilian | River | SYDNEY | DIP | 2800 | 37 | 2009-05-12 | 3 |

```
-- Note! Wrong result!
SELECT fname, lname, city, education, salary
FROM employee
WHERE city = 'LONDON'
AND salary = 2800 OR education = 'Ba''
```

| FNAME | LNAME | CITY | EDUCATION | SALARY |
|-------|-------|------|-----------|--------|
| Peter | Stream | LONDON | Ba | 2800 |
| Leon | Lake | LONDON | NULL | 2800 |
| Laura | Brown | SYDNEY | Ba | 2650 |

The result set includes Laura Brown from SYDNEY, although we were only supposed to be looking at Londoners. The query returns all London employees that make 2800 and all employees with education Ba, independent of salary or city. You can think of the OR condition as being evaluated independently.

To get the desired result, we must use parentheses:

```
SELECT fname, lname, city, education, salary
FROM employee
WHERE city = 'LONDON'
AND (salary = 2800 OR education = 'Ba')
```

| FNAME | LNAME | CITY | EDUCATION | SALARY |
|-------|-------|------|-----------|--------|
| Peter | Stream | LONDON | Ba | 2800 |
| Leon | Lake | LONDON | NULL | 2800 |

Now the query returns London employees with either 2800 salary or Ba degree.

 It is easy to make mistakes in queries containing both AND and OR conditions. Tip: **if a query contains both AND and OR conditions, always use parentheses in the WHERE clause.** They will also make your query easier to read. It is good to use parenthesis whenever they are appropriate.

The figure below shows where you should put the parentheses. They should be placed around the conditions that are combined with OR.

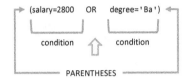

Figure 12: where you should put the parentheses.

## EXERCISES

1.  Get the first and last names of employees that have the degree 'Ba'.

2.  Which employees have a salary that is less than 2960; get the columns first name, last name, and salary.

3.  Include in the previous also the employee with the salary 2960; order by salary from highest to lowest.

4.  Search for employees of department 3 (deptno column in employee table) that are stationed in London. Return first name, last name, city and department number. Order by last name and first name.

5.  We want both Londoners and those that have a salary of 2800: empno, first and last names, city and salary.

---

## 6.3 String Searches

You can do string searches with partial matches using the LIKE operator. There are two special characters:

%   (percent) a wildcard symbol that represents zero, one or multiple characters

_   (underscore) represents a single character

*List all employees whose last name starts with the letter B. Fetch columns last name, empno and city, order by last name.*

```
SELECT lname, empno, city
FROM employee
WHERE lname LIKE 'B%'
ORDER BY lname

LNAME      EMPNO      CITY
--------   ----------------
Brooke     2245       HELSINKI
Brown      3546       SYDNEY
```

*List all employees whose second character of their empno is 2.*

```
SELECT empno, fname, lname
FROM   employee
WHERE  empno LIKE '_2%'

EMPNO      FNAME      LNAME
--------   --------   --------
2245       Rachel     Brooke
2234       Mike       Wood
```

*List all projects with the string 'TI' in the name.*

```
SELECT project_name
FROM project
WHERE project_name LIKE '%TI%'

PROJECT_NAME
----------------
STATISTICS
ACCOUNTING
```

A project named TI would have also been included.

You can also exclude results, by using NOT LIKE.

*Search for projects that don't have the letter U in their name.*

```
SELECT project_name
FROM project
WHERE project_name NOT LIKE '%U%'

PROJECT_NAME
-----------------
BOOKKEEPING
STATISTICS
BILLING
```

You can also use the following format:

```
WHERE NOT project_name LIKE '%U%'
```

## BETWEEN and IN

The BETWEEN operator selects values within a given range. The BETWEEN operator is inclusive: begin and end values are included.

*Select employees whose tax rate is between 24.5 and 32. Order by tax rate.*

```
SELECT fname, lname, tax_rate
FROM employee
WHERE tax_rate BETWEEN 24.5 AND 32
ORDER BY tax_rate

FNAME      LNAME        TAX_RATE
--------   ----------   ----------
Leon       Lake         24.5
Rachel     Brooke       31
Peter      Taylor       31
```

*Select employees whose tax rate is **not** between 24.5 and 32. Order by tax rate.*

```
SELECT fname, lname, tax_rate
FROM employee
WHERE tax_rate NOT BETWEEN 24.5 AND 32
ORDER BY tax_rate
```

```
FNAME       LNAME           TAX_RATE
--------    ----------      ----------
Laura       Brown           22
Peter       Stream          22
Mike        Wood            33
Lilian      River           37
```

The IN operator is a shorthand for multiple OR conditions.

*Select all employees whose tax rate is one of the following: 24.5, 31, or 37.*

```
SELECT fname, lname, tax_rate
FROM employee
WHERE tax_rate = 24.5
OR tax_rate = 31
OR tax_rate = 37
```

```
FNAME       LNAME           TAX_RATE
------------------------    ----------
Rachel      Brooke          31
Leon        Lake            24.5
Peter       Taylor          31
Lilian      River           37
```

The previous query can be simplified using the IN -operator:

```
SELECT fname, lname, tax_rate
FROM employee
WHERE tax_rate IN (24.5, 31, 37)
```

You can also use **NOT IN**:

```
SELECT fname, lname, tax_rate
FROM employee
WHERE tax_rate NOT IN (24.5, 31, 37)
```

| FNAME | LNAME | TAX_RATE |
| ------- | --------- | ---------- |
| Peter | Stream | 22 |
| Mike | Wood | 33 |
| Laura | Brown | 22 |

or

```
WHERE NOT tax_rate IN (24.5, 31, 37)
```

The list in the IN-operator can contain numeric constants, string constants, or dates. Strings and dates are delimited by single quotes.

## NULL

SQL has a special notation for a value that is missing: NULL. NULL is not a blank, a zero, or a string of zero length (note the exception at the end of this chapter). If no value is given to a column during INSERT, it will obtain the "value" NULL (as long as the column has not been defined as NOT NULL during the creation of the table).

The easiest way to understand NULL is to think of it as an unknown value. That is, its value could be anything. If the salary is zero, we know that no salary has been paid. If the salary is NULL, we know that it is missing, or the information has not yet been stored in the table (and could be anything).

A column with a NULL is retrieved using **IS** instead of equal (=), as in the following example.

*List employees that are missing a degree. Retrieve name, city, and degree.*

```
SELECT fname, lname, city, education
FROM employee
WHERE education IS NULL


FNAME  LNAME  CITY    EDUCATION
-----  -----  ------  ---------
Leon   Lake   LONDON  NULL
```

In your database management system, NULL might show up as a blank (Oracle, Snowflake, PostgreSQL, and DB2) or as the word NULL (SQL Server and MySQL). If the columns A and B are both NULL the result of WHERE A = B is false. We can't assume that two unknowns would be equal. It may be counterintuitive that the following query does not return the project P6 STATISTICS, whose priority does not equal 2.

*List all projects where priority differs from two.*

| projno | project_name | priority | location |
|--------|--------------|----------|----------|
| P1 | BOOKKEEPING | 2 | LONDON |
| **P2** | **BILLING** | **1** | **HELSINKI** |
| **P3** | **WAREHOUSING** | **3** | **HELSINKI** |
| P4 | ACCOUNTING | 2 | LONDON |
| **P5** | **CUSTOMERS** | **3** | **SINGAPORE** |
| P6 | STATISTICS | NULL | NULL |

```
SELECT *
FROM project
WHERE priority <> 2


PROJNO  PROJECT_NAME  PRIORITY  LOCATION
------  ------------  --------  -----------
P2      BILLING           1     HELSINKI
P3      WAREHOUSING       3     HELSINKI
P5      CUSTOMERS         3     SINGAPORE
```

The explanation for this behavior is that because the priority of project P6 is unknown, it *could* be two, so it is left out of the result set. If you want to include project P6 in the result, use the following query:

```
SELECT *
FROM project
WHERE priority <> 2
OR priority IS NULL          -- or use COALESCE
```

| PROJNO | PROJECT_NAME | PRIORITY | LOCATION |
| --- | --- | --- | --- |
| P2 | BILLING | 1 | HELSINKI |
| P3 | WAREHOUSING | 3 | HELSINKI |
| P5 | CUSTOMERS | 3 | SINGAPORE |
| P6 | STATISTICS | NULL | NULL |

In Oracle, a zero-length string (") behaves like NULL. This is unfortunate and different from other products. According to Oracle Corporation, this may change in future releases.

The next chapter will show how NULL behaves with different functions. The end of the chapter will give some examples of useful NULL functions.

## EXERCISES

1. Get all columns for employees that don't have a salary of 2800.

2. Find employees in department 3 who are from Sydney or have a tax rate of 22.

3. Find employees with education 'Ba' or 'Ma' and salary of 3100 or 2800.

4. Find projects that start with the letter 'B', get all columns.

5. Find employees with cities that have the letter 'I' in them. Get columns empno, lname, fname, city, and salary.

6. Find employees whose second letter in last name is not 'a'. Get columns empno, fname and lname.

7. Search for employees whose tax rate is between 22 and 31 (including those values). Use the BETWEEN operator. Order by tax rate.

8. Find employees whose tax rate is 31, 24.5, or 37 (use IN).

9. Find employees with a missing education (IS NULL).

10. Find employees whose education is not MA.

---

## 6.4 Functions

### Aggregate Functions

We introduce the five most used aggregate functions. They can be used to calculate sums, averages, minimums, and maximums of numeric columns and to count the number of rows in a result set.

```
AVG        average
SUM        sum
MIN        minimum value
MAX        maximum value
COUNT      number of values
```

Let's first look at some queries with only aggregate functions in the SELECT list. Note that these queries don't return individual rows as the queries previously in this chapter. An aggregate function calculates a single value from a set of values, such as a sum of the values or their average.

*Find the maximum, minimum, and average salary.*

| empno | fname | lname | city | education | salary | tax_rate | start_date | deptno |
|-------|-------|-------|------|-----------|--------|----------|------------|--------|
| 2134 | Peter | Stream | LONDON | Ba | 2800 | 22 | 2020-03-02 | 3 |
| 2234 | Mike | Wood | LONDON | PhD | 3100 | 33 | 2009-10-15 | 1 |
| 2245 | Rachel | Brooke | HELSINKI | MA | 3100 | 31 | 2014-09-24 | 4 |
| 2345 | Leon | Lake | LONDON | NULL | 2800 | 24.5 | 2018-01-01 | 3 |
| 2884 | Peter | Taylor | HELSINKI | MA | 2960 | 31 | 2009-05-12 | NULL |
| 3546 | Laura | Brown | SYDNEY | Ba | 2650 | 22 | 2017-09-15 | 1 |
| 3547 | Lilian | River | SYDNEY | DIP | 2800 | 37 | 2009-05-12 | 3 |

```
SELECT MAX(salary) AS max,
       MIN(salary) AS min,
       AVG(salary) AS ave
FROM employee
```

```
    MAX         MIN         AVE
---------- ---------- ----------
   3100        2650   2887.14286
```

*How many employees are there in project P4?*

```
SELECT COUNT(*) AS cnt
FROM proj_emp
WHERE projno = 'P4'
```

```
   CNT
----------
     3
```

*How many hours have been spent in total?*

```
SELECT SUM(hours_act) AS total
FROM proj_emp
```

```
TOTAL
----------
4100
```

Note that NULLs are not counted in the result.

*How many cities do our employees come from?*

```
SELECT COUNT(DISTINCT city) AS city_count
FROM employee

CITY_COUNT
----------
         3
```

COUNT(DISTINCT …) will not count NULLs. If you want to include them in the count, you must use the COALESCE function (see Chapter 18.1, COALESCE NULL function).

*How many projects are there?*

```
SELECT COUNT(*) AS cnt
FROM project

       cnt
----------
         6
```

COUNT(*) will give you the number of rows that satisfy the search condition. Note, that the rows can have columns with NULL. So COUNT(*) ignores NULLs.

*How many projects are there that have a known priority?*

```
SELECT COUNT(priority) AS cnt
FROM project

  cnt
-----
    5
```

COUNT(column) will give you the number of values that differ from NULL. The query can also be expressed as follows:

```
SELECT COUNT(*) AS cnt
FROM project
WHERE priority IS NOT NULL
```

NULLs do not participate in calculating the result of the functions SUM, AVG, MAX, MIN, or COUNT(column). For example, AVG(hours_est) does not take NULLs into consideration. It calculates the real average using known values. COUNT(*) calculates the number of rows regardless of the possible NULL values in one or several columns of the rows.

Here are some rules for aggregate functions:

- You can't use aggregate functions in the WHERE clause.
- In the HAVING clause, you mostly use aggregate functions.
- If aggregate functions and "regular" columns are in the same SELECT list, you must use grouping (GROUP BY). See Chapter 6.6 GROUPING.

```
SELECT lname, fname, tax_rate
FROM employee                         -- This will cause
WHERE tax_rate = MIN(tax_rate)        -- an error message!
```

You can't use aggregate functions in the WHERE clause! We will solve this problem later (see Subqueries).

If you need rounding when summing values, be careful! Your result will differ depending on when you do the rounding. For our example, we will calculate the daily salary with the formula salary/30. This will give us values such as 93,3333333 and 98,6666667.

Let's calculate the sum of the daily salaries by applying the rounding before and after summing the values. The results differ since the first query will calculate the sum with rounded, unprecise values, and the second query will calculate the sum with exact values and do the rounding at the end.

```
SELECT SUM(ROUND(salary/30, 1)) AS total
FROM employee

TOTAL
----------
673,5

SELECT ROUND(SUM(salary/30), 1) AS total
FROM employee

TOTAL
----------
673,7
```

There are many other functions in SQL products that you can use in the SELECT list and in WHERE and HAVING clauses. Some have been standardized, but many are product-specific. We present some of the most important ones here, and many more examples can be found in Chapter 20. Check your product's user guide for other available functions.

### String Functions

In this chapter, we introduce some of the most common string functions. You can then familiarize yourself with the other string functions available in your own product.

*Extract three characters from the last name, starting in position 2.*

In SQL Server, we will use the function SUBSTRING, also in Snowflake, PostgreSQL, MySQL, and Hive:

```
SELECT lname, SUBSTRING(lname, 2, 3) AS part
FROM employee
ORDER BY lname

LNAME       PART
---------   ----
Brooke      roo
Brown       row
Lake        ake
River       ive
Stream      tre
Taylor      ayl
Wood        ood
```

So the parameters are: SUBSTRING(lname, 2, 3), where 2 = starting position and 3 = length.

Use **SUBSTR** in Oracle and DB2. You can also use it in Snowflake, MySQL, PostgreSQL, and Hive.

```
SELECT lname, SUBSTR(lname, 2, 3) AS part
FROM employee
ORDER BY lname
```

We want to get three characters from left or right (does not work in Oracle or Hive):

```
LEFT(lname, 3)      RIGHT(lname, 3)
```

In Oracle and Hive, you can get the last three characters using a negative start position (take the third last position and three characters from there):

```
SUBSTR(lname, -3, 3)
```

Converting to upper or lower case:

```
SELECT UPPER(lname) AS name_uc, lname,
       LOWER(city) AS city_lc, city
FROM employee


NAME_UC      LNAME        CITY_LC      CITY
----------   ----------   ----------   ----------
STREAM       Stream       london       LONDON
WOOD         Wood         london       LONDON
BROOKE       Brooke       helsinki     HELSINKI
LAKE         Lake         london       LONDON
TAYLOR       Taylor       helsinki     HELSINKI
BROWN        Brown        SYDNEY       SYDNEY
RIVER        River        SYDNEY       SYDNEY
```

Let's fetch employees named Brooke regardless of case, meaning both BROOKE and Brooke are returned. You don't need this in SQL Server or MySQL, as they are case-insensitive by default.

```
SELECT lname, fname, empno, salary
FROM employee
WHERE UPPER(lname) = 'BROOKE'


lname     fname      empno      salary
-------   --------   -------    -------
Brooke    Rachel     2245       3100.00
```

Note. The above statement might be slow to execute because it contains a function in the WHERE clause and hence might inhibit the usage of an index on lname.

Calculate the length of a string with the **LENGTH** function:

```
SELECT lname,
       LENGTH(lname) AS lname_len   -- In SQL Server use LEN
FROM employee

LNAME           LNAME_LEN
----------      ----------
Stream                  6
Wood                    4
Brooke                  6
Lake                    4
Taylor                  6
Brown                   5
River                   5
```

In SQL Server, use LEN (lname) instead. It works in Snowflake, too. In Oracle and DB2, if a column has been defined as CHAR, it will always be filled up with blanks to the full length of the column. For instance, the data type of education is CHAR(8). If the column is given the value 'Ba    ', it will be saved as 'Ba' in the database. There will be six filler blanks at the end of the string and the length will always be eight. To find the actual length of the string in Oracle and DB2, you must first remove the trailing blanks with the RTRIM function:

```
SELECT lname, education, LENGTH(education) col_len,
       LENGTH(RTRIM(education)) AS value_len
FROM employee

LNAME           EDUCATION   COL_LEN   VALUE_LEN
----------      ----------  -------   ----------
Stream          Ba                8           2
Wood            PhD               8           3
Brooke          MA                8           2
Lake            NULL           NULL        NULL
Taylor          MA                8           2
Brown           Ba                8           2
River           DIP               8           3
```

To combine strings, concatenate them with the double-pipe operator (||) in Oracle, Snowflake, PostgreSQL and DB2. For example:

```
SELECT lname || ', '  || city AS name_city
FROM employee
WHERE empno IN ('2134', '2245')

NAME_CITY
----------------------
Stream, LONDON
Brooke, HELSINKI
```

We used a literal string ', ' in the SELECT list, and it appears as such in every row. The column lname is a varchar, so the comma will come directly after the name (no spaces). If you combine the column education (CHAR(8)) and lname, there will be spaces between them. For instance:

```
"Ba      Stream"
```

You can remove the trailing blanks with the **RTRIM** function.

> **SQL Server concatenation**

In SQL Server, use the plus sign + instead of || to concatenate strings:

```
SELECT  lname + ', ' +  city AS name_city
FROM employee
WHERE empno IN ('2134', '2245')

NAME_CITY
----------------------
Stream, LONDON
Brooke, HELSINKI
```

You can also concatenate strings using the CONCAT function, by concatenating two or more strings at a time (in DB2 only two). You must use this function for concatenation in Hive and MySQL. The following query will give you the same answer as the previous ones.

MySQL and Hive:

```
SELECT CONCAT(lname, ', ', city) AS name_city
FROM employee
WHERE empno IN ('2134', '2245')
```

In DB2, you can use CONCAT also like this:

```
SELECT  lname CONCAT ', ' CONCAT  city AS name_city
  FROM employee
```

The space character can be removed from the left with LTRIM and from the right RTRIM. You can remove from both ends using TRIM:

```
SELECT LTRIM ('  left') AS ltest,
       RTRIM('right  ') AS rtest,
       TRIM('  middle  ') AS mtest


ltest   rtest     mtest
-------  -------   ------
left     right     middle
```

## Numeric Functions

Decimals are rounded with the ROUND function. In the following query, we round the daily salary to one decimal (for instance, 0.14 rounds to 0.1 and 0.15 rounds to 0.2). Try:

```
SELECT lname, salary, ROUND(salary/30,2) AS daily_rate
FROM employee
WHERE lname = 'Brown'


lname    salary     daily_rate
------   --------    ----------
Brown    2650.00     88.33
```

SQL Server rounds but does not cut zeroes from the end. Use CAST instead:

```
SELECT lname, salary,
       CAST(salary/30 AS DECIMAL (7,2)) AS daily_rate
FROM employee
WHERE lname = 'Brown'


lname    salary     daily_rate
------   --------   ----------
Brown    2650.00    88.33
```

Sometimes rounding up or down to the nearest integer is required. It can be done using FLOOR and CEILING functions. In Oracle, Hive and Snowflake use CEIL instead of CEILING.

```
SELECT lname, tax_rate,
FLOOR(tax_rate) AS to_floor,
CEILING(tax_rate) AS to_ceil  -- Oracle, Hive, Snowflake: CEIL
FROM employee
WHERE lname = 'Lake'


lname    tax_rate   to_floor     to_ceil
------   --------   ----------   --------
Lake     24.5       24           25
```

There are plenty of other numeric functions available (see Chapter 20). Refer to your product manual for more information.

## Restricting the Number of Rows Returned

Sometimes, you just want to read a couple of rows from a table just to get an idea of what is in it. In Oracle, especially when using the SQL*Plus-interface, use the reserved word ROWNUM, which gives the sequence number of the row. For instance, to see three rows from the beginning of the table:

In Oracle:

```
SELECT *
 FROM proj_emp
 WHERE ROWNUM < 4
```

| PROJNO | EMPNO | HOURS_ACT | HOURS_EST |
|--------|-------|-----------|-----------|
| P1 | 2134 | 300 | 300 |
| P1 | 2245 | 200 | 300 |
| P1 | 3546 | 400 | 500 |

In SQL Server:

```
SELECT TOP 3 *
   FROM proj_emp
```

In Snowflake, PostgreSQL, MySQL and Hive:

```
SELECT *
   FROM proj_emp
   LIMIT 3
```

In DB2, Oracle, PostgreSQL and Snowflake:

```
SELECT *
   FROM proj_emp
   FETCH FIRST 3 ROWS ONLY
```

## EXERCISES

1. Find the lowest and highest priority. Give alias names min_prio and max_prio.

2. How many projects are there in the project table?

3. What is the average tax rate? Set 'avg_tax' as column header (alias name).

4. How much is the total salary of all employees? Column heading salary_total (alias name).

5. How many different educations are there in the employee table? Column heading edu_cnt.

6. Get three first characters (letters) of each employee's last name.

7. Combine the last and first names of the employees so that they look similar to this: Wood, Mike. The column heading (alias name) is 'name'.

8. The user id for employees is generated by combining the first two letters of the last name and first name and by capitalizing them. For example, Mike Wood will get the user id WOMI. Use column heading 'user_id'. Generate the user id for all employees. Include columns lname and fname for easier checking.

---

## 6.5 Dates

Handling dates is quite tricky because the format of dates is affected by country-specific settings in the products and interfaces. We are using the ISO date standard, which is also the ANSI SQL -standard:

```
yyyy-mm-dd (e.g. 2024-09-26)
```

This is the native date format in MySQL, SQL Server, Snowflake, and PostgreSQL.

In different parts of the world, dates are presented in other formats. We will give examples later.

The American format is mm/dd/yyyy. In Europe, the typical format is dd.mm.yyyy. China, Japan, and South Korea use yyyy-mm-dd. In Australia, the format is dd/mm/yyyy as well as in some South Asian countries. Because it is easy to get confused with the different formats and make mistakes, we will show the best ways to use dates in each product.

There are several product-specific functions that you can use to, for example, calculate the number of days between two dates or extract the year, month, or day from a date (the YEAR, MONTH, and DAY functions). There are also find functions for finding the weekday or handling timestamps.

The current day is available with the ANSI-standard keyword CURRENT_DATE. In SQL Server, many use the GETDATE() function. Oracle users are used to the function SYSDATE, which is similar to CURRENT_DATE. (Oracle CURRENT_DATE returns the date on the client and SYSDATE returns the date on the server side).

If you just want to get the current date, do the following:

| | |
|---|---|
| **MySQL** | `SELECT CURRENT_DATE` |
| | `SELECT CURDATE()` |
| **DB2** | `SELECT CURRENT_DATE FROM` |
| | `sysibm.sysdummy1` |
| | `SELECT CURRENT DATE FROM` |
| | `sysibm.sysdummy1` |
| **Oracle** | `SELECT CURRENT_DATE` |
| | `SELECT SYSDATE` |
| **SQL Server** | `SELECT GETDATE()  --or SYSDATETIME()` |
| | `SELECT CURRENT_DATE` |
| **Hive** | `SELECT FROM_UNIXTIME(UNIX_TIMESTAMP())` |
| **Snowflake, PostgreSQL** | `SELECT CURRENT_DATE` |

DB2 does not support a SELECT statement without a FROM clause. Therefore, the ready-made, single-row 'sysibm.sysdummy1' table is used to retrieve the date. In older versions of Oracle, we use the 'dual' table for the same purpose. For example, all other products can have a SELECT clause without FROM to retrieve this date.

To find out how the date is presented in your country and the product you are using, use the examples in the table above.

CURRENT_TIMESTAMP will give you both the date and the time.

In Oracle, you get both the date and time this way:

```
SELECT TO_CHAR(SYSDATE,'DD.MM.YYYY HH24:MI:SS') AS ts

TS
-------------------
24.09.2024 12:05:41
```

 Reminder! Pay special attention to the numbers for weeks and weekdays. Check your product manual for detailed information.

Let's look at the product-specific basics of date processing next.

## Dates in Oracle

The safest way to handle a date in Oracle is to use the TO_DATE function:

```
SELECT lname, fname,
       TO_CHAR(start_date, 'YYYY-MM-DD') AS start_date
FROM employee
WHERE start_date = TO_DATE('2009-05-12', 'YYYY-MM-DD')

LNAME     FNAME   START_DATE
--------  ------- ----------
Taylor    Peter   2009-05-12
River     Lilian  2009-05-12
```

In your country, you can get the date in the right format without a TO_CHAR function (if the Oracle parameters are set right):

```
SELECT lname, fname, start_date
FROM   ...
```

The other option for the WHERE clause is the ANSI-compliant DATE function:

```
WHERE start_date = DATE '2009-05-12'.
```

If your version of Oracle is installed correctly, you can use your own local format. For instance, in Europe, typically you can write:

```
WHERE start_date = '12.5.2009'
```

However, the TO_DATE or DATE functions work everywhere.

The Oracle data type DATE includes time. If it is not given on insert or update, the date column will only include the date, and the time will be zero. The following statement will save both date and time from SYSDATE (current day and time) in the start_date column:

```
INSERT INTO employee (empno, lname, start_date)
VALUES ('8768','Bean', SYSDATE)      --date + time included
```

Let's take a look at the resulting row (the day of the insert was 2024-10-08):

```
SELECT empno, lname,
   TO_CHAR(start_date, 'YYYY-MM-DD HH24:MI') AS start_date_time
 FROM employee
 WHERE empno = '8768'

EMPNO   LNAME        START_DATE_TIME
-----   ----------   -----------------
8768    Bean         2024-10-08 19:28
```

The column includes time, which we formatted using the TO_CHAR function. Let's look at this query:

```
SELECT empno, lname,
  TO_CHAR(start_date, 'YYYY-MM-DD') AS start_date,
  TO_CHAR (start_date, 'YYYY-MM-DD HH24:MI') AS start_date_time
FROM employee
WHERE start_date = TO_DATE('2024-10-08', 'YYYY-MM-DD')
```

No rows were returned! We have to use the TRUNC function:

```
SELECT empno, lname,
  TO_CHAR(start_date, 'YYYY-MM-DD') AS start_date,
  TO_CHAR (start_date, 'YYYY-MM-DD HH24:MI') AS start_date_time
FROM employee
WHERE TRUNC(start_date) = TO_DATE('2024-10-08', 'YYYY-MM-DD')


EMPNO   LNAME        START_DATE_  START_DATE_TIME
-----   ----------   ----------   ----------------
8768    Bean         2024-10-08   2024-10-08 19:42
```

If the date is saved without the time component, no TRUNC function is necessary in SELECT. So, if we had inserted the new row into the employee table using the following statement, there would be no need for the TRUNC –function in the query.

```
INSERT INTO employee (empno, lname, start_date)
VALUES ('8768','Bean', TRUNC(SYSDATE))    --time is not included
```

> The TRUNC function will prevent the use of an index specified on the date column. If the table is large and you need to often query dates you might get a performance hit. In that case consider creating an Oracle function-based index for the date column.

Oracle has handy functions for dates such as LAST_DAY, NEXT_DAY, ADD_MONTHS, and MONTHS_BETWEEN.

In finding the difference between two dates, the TRUNC function will round off decimals resulting from differing times of day:

```
SELECT lname,
    TO_CHAR(start_date, 'YYYY-MM-DD') AS start_date,
    TO_CHAR(SYSDATE, 'YYYY-MM-DD') AS today,
    TRUNC(SYSDATE  - start_date)  AS diff
FROM employee
```

```
LNAME      START_DATE  TODAY       DIFF
--------   ----------  ----------  ----
Stream     2020-03-02  2024-10-08  1681
Wood       2009-10-15  2024-10-08  5472
Brooke     2014-09-24  2024-10-08  3667
Lake       2018-01-01  2024-10-08  2472
Taylor     2009-05-12  2024-10-08  5628
Brown      2017-09-15  2024-10-08  2580
River      2009-05-12  2024-10-08  5628
```

You can retrieve parts of the date with the EXTRACT function (TO_CHAR also works):

```
SELECT lname,
        TO_CHAR(start_date, 'YYYY-MM-DD') AS start_date,
        EXTRACT (YEAR FROM start_date) AS hire_year,
        EXTRACT (MONTH FROM start_date) AS mon,
        EXTRACT (DAY FROM start_date) AS day
FROM employee
```

```
LNAME      START_DATE  HIRE_YEAR   MON   DAY
-------    ----------  ----------  ----  ---
Stream     2020-03-02        2020  3     2
Wood       2009-10-15        2009  10    15
Brooke     2014-09-24        2014  9     24
Lake       2018-01-01        2018  1     1
Taylor     2009-05-12        2009  5     12
Brown      2017-09-15        2017  9     15
River      2009-05-12        2009  5     12
```

## Dates in SQL Server

The internal format of a date in SQL Server is yyyy-mm-dd.

```
SELECT lname, fname, start_date
FROM employee
WHERE start_date = '2009-05-12'

lname      fname       start_date
------     -----       -----------------------
Taylor     Peter       2009-05-12 00:00:00.000
River      Lilian      2009-05-12 00:00:00.000
```

You can get the format of your country (if it is different from the above) by using the FORMAT function (e.g., the USA -format). We show here two methods:

```
SELECT lname, fname,
    start_date,
    FORMAT (start_date, 'MM/dd/yyyy') AS USA_Date,   -- capital M
    FORMAT (start_date, 'd', 'en-US') AS USA_Date2
FROM employee
WHERE start_date = '2009-05-12'

lname      fname    start_date                USA_Date       USA_Date2
--------   ------   -----------------------   ------------   ---------
Taylor     Peter    2009-05-12 00:00:00.000   05/12/2009     5/12/2009
River      Lilian   2009-05-12 00:00:00.000   05/12/2009     5/12/2009
```

Use capital M in the date mask (m is for minutes). The 'en-US' text is the so-called culture in the FORMAT function. You can find your country's codes from a list by googling "SQL Server 2012 FORMAT String Function Culture".

Here is another example of the FORMAT function, this time in Germany:

```
SELECT lname, fname,
     FORMAT(start_date,'D','de') AS long,    --date (de), text
     FORMAT(start_date,'d','de') AS normal, --date (de), date
     FORMAT(start_date,'yyyyMMdd') AS dense
FROM employee
```

```
lname   fname  long                         normal      dense
------- -----  ---------------------------  ----------  --------
Stream  Peter  Montag, 2. März 2020         02.03.2020  20200302
Wood    Mike   Donnerstag, 15. Oktober 2009 15.10.2009  20091015
Brooke  Rachel Mittwoch, 24. September 2014 24.09.2014  20140924
Lake    Leon   Montag, 1. Januar 2018       01.01.2018  20180101
Taylor  Peter  Dienstag, 12. Mai 2009       12.05.2009  20090512
Brown   Laura  Freitag, 15. September 2017  15.09.2017  20170915
River   Lilian Dienstag, 12. Mai 2009       12.05.2009  20090512
```

Warning: don't use the format dd.mm.yyyy, for instance, WHERE start_date = '5.12.2009'. You may get an incorrect result! If you want to use that format, use the function FORMAT:

```
WHERE FORMAT (start_date, 'dd.MM.yyyy') = '5.12.2009'
```

The FORMAT function can be used to extract parts from a date:

```
SELECT lname, start_date,
     FORMAT (start_date, 'yy') AS yr,
     FORMAT (start_date, 'MM') AS mon,
     FORMAT (start_date, 'dd') AS day
FROM employee
```

```
lname    start_date               yr     mon  day
-------  ----------------------  -----  ---  ---
Stream   2020-03-02 00:00:00.000  2020   03   02
Wood     2009-10-15 00:00:00.000  2009   10   15
Brooke   2014-09-24 00:00:00.000  2014   09   24
Lake     2018-01-01 00:00:00.000  2018   01   01
Taylor   2009-05-12 00:00:00.000  2009   05   12
Brown    2017-09-15 00:00:00.000  2017   09   15
River    2009-05-12 00:00:00.000  2009   05   12
```

The DATEADD function can be used to calculate a new date by adding a certain number of days to a given date. The example using DATEDIFF shows how to calculate the days between the start_date in the employee table and the current date. As shown, the query has been run on 17.6.2020:

```
SELECT lname, start_date, GETDATE() AS today,
       DATEDIFF(dd, start_date, GETDATE()) AS diff
FROM employee
```

| Lname | start_date | today | diff |
|--------|-------------------------|--------------------------|------|
| Stream | 2020-03-02 00:00:00.000 | 2024-10-09 14:37:10.787 | 1681 |
| Wood   | 2009-10-15 00:00:00.000 | 2024-10-09 14:37:10.787 | 5472 |
| Brooke | 2014-09-24 00:00:00.000 | 2024-10-09 14:37:10.787 | 3667 |
| Lake   | 2018-01-01 00:00:00.000 | 2024-10-09 14:37:10.787 | 2472 |
| Taylor | 2009-05-12 00:00:00.000 | 2024-10-09 14:37:10.787 | 5628 |
| Brown  | 2017-09-15 00:00:00.000 | 2024-10-09 14:37:10.787 | 2580 |
| River  | 2009-05-12 00:00:00.000 | 2024-10-09 14:37:10.787 | 5628 |

*Dates in DB2*

The format of the date in DB2 depends on the installation parameters. Here we use the ANSI standard yyyy-mm-dd:

```
SELECT lname, fname, start_date
FROM employee
WHERE VARCHAR_FORMAT (date_col,'YYYY-MM-DD') = '2009-05-12'
```

| lname | fname | start_date |
|--------|--------|------------|
| Taylor | Peter | 2009-05-12 |
| River | Lilian | 2009-05-12 |

DB2 has lots of functions to extract parts out of dates, such as:

**DAY, MONTH, YEAR, DAYNAME, YEAR, MONTHNAME, DAYOFYEAR, MONTHS_BETWEEN**

Let's give it a try:

```
SELECT lname,
       VARCHAR_FORMAT (start_date, 'YYYY-MM-DD') AS start_date,
       YEAR(start_date) AS yr,
       MONTH(start_date) AS mon,
       DAY(start_date) AS day
FROM employee
```

| LNAME | START_DATE | YR | MON | DAY |
|-------|-----------|------|-----|-----|
| Stream | 2020-03-02 | 2020 | 3 | 2 |
| Wood | 2009-10-15 | 2009 | 10 | 15 |
| Brooke | 2014-09-24 | 2014 | 9 | 24 |
| Lake | 2018-01-01 | 2018 | 1 | 1 |
| Taylor | 2009-05-12 | 2009 | 5 | 12 |
| Brown | 2017-09-15 | 2017 | 9 | 15 |
| River | 2009-05-12 | 2009 | 5 | 12 |

Calculate the date difference between the current date and start_date. This query was run on 2024-10-08:

```
SELECT lname,
       VARCHAR_FORMAT (start_date, 'YYYY-MM-DD') AS start_date
       VARCHAR_FORMAT (CURRENT DATE, 'YYYY-MM-DD') AS today
       DAYS(CURRENT DATE) - DAYS(start_date) AS diff
FROM employee
```

| LNAME | START_DATE | TODAY | DIFF |
|-------|-----------|-------|------|
| Stream | 2020-03-02 | 2024-10-08 | 1681 |
| Wood | 2009-10-15 | 2024-10-08 | 5472 |
| Brooke | 2014-09-24 | 2024-10-08 | 3667 |
| Lake | 2018-01-01 | 2024-10-08 | 2472 |
| Taylor | 2009-05-12 | 2024-10-08 | 5628 |
| Brown | 2017-09-15 | 2024-10-08 | 2580 |
| River | 2009-05-12 | 2024-10-08 | 5628 |

*Dates in MySQL*

In MySQL, dates are given in the format yyyy-mm-dd, we also present this time in the Australian date format:

```
SELECT lname, fname,
       start_date,
       DATE_FORMAT(start_date, '%d/%m/%Y') AS Australian_day
FROM employee
WHERE start_date = '2009-05-12'
```

| lname  | fname  | start_date          | Australian_day |
|--------|--------|---------------------|----------------|
| Taylor | Peter  | 2009-05-12 00:00:00 | 12/05/2009     |
| River  | Lilian | 2009-05-12 00:00:00 | 12/05/2009     |

The parameter %d means days, %m months, and %Y years in four characters. Consult the MySQL manual for more formatting options. Date parts are extracted from dates using the EXTRACT function (as in Oracle) or using the method below:

```
SELECT lname, start_date,
       YEAR(start_date) AS yr,
       MONTH(start_date) AS mon,
       DAY(start_date) AS day
FROM employee
```

| lname  | start_date          | yr   | mon | day |
|--------|---------------------|------|-----|-----|
| Stream | 2020-03-02 00:00:00 | 2020 | 3   | 2   |
| Wood   | 2009-10-15 00:00:00 | 2009 | 10  | 15  |
| Brooke | 2014-09-24 00:00:00 | 2014 | 9   | 24  |
| Lake   | 2018-01-01 00:00:00 | 2018 | 1   | 1   |
| Taylor | 2009-05-12 00:00:00 | 2009 | 5   | 12  |
| Brown  | 2017-09-15 00:00:00 | 2017 | 9   | 15  |
| River  | 2009-05-12 00:00:00 | 2009 | 5   | 12  |

We calculate the differences between dates using the DATEADD and DATEDIFF functions. Let's calculate the difference between today and start_date as of 17.6.2020:

```
SELECT lname, start_date,
       CURRENT_DATE AS today,
       DATEDIFF(CURRENT_DATE, start_date) AS diff
FROM employee
```

```
lname     start_date            today        diff
-------   -------------------   ----------   ----
Stream    2020-03-02 00:00:00   2024-10-09   1682
Wood      2009-10-15 00:00:00   2024-10-09   5473
Brooke    2014-09-24 00:00:00   2024-10-09   3668
Lake      2018-01-01 00:00:00   2024-10-09   2473
Taylor    2009-05-12 00:00:00   2024-10-09   5629
Brown     2017-09-15 00:00:00   2024-10-09   2581
River     2009-05-12 00:00:00   2024-10-09   5629
```

### Dates in PostgreSQL

In PostgreSQL, dates are given in the format yyyy-mm-dd:

```
SELECT lname, fname, start_date,
       TO_CHAR(start_date, 'DD.MM.YYYY') AS eur_date
FROM employee
WHERE start_date = '2009-05-12'
```

```
lname     fname     start_date
-------   -----     ----------
Taylor    Peter     2009-05-12
River     Lilian    2009-05-12
```

The column on the right will give you start_date in the usual European format.

In search conditions, you can also use the following:

```
WHERE start_date = TO_DATE('2009-05-12', 'DD.MM.YYYY')
WHERE start_date = DATE '2009-05-12'
```

Parts of the date can be extracted like this:

```
SELECT lname, start_date,
       EXTRACT (YEAR FROM start_date) AS yr,
       EXTRACT (MONTH FROM start_date) AS mon,
       EXTRACT (DAY FROM start_date) AS day
FROM employee
```

| lname | start_date | yr | mon | day |
|-------|-----------|------|-----|-----|
| Stream | 2020-03-02 | 2020 | 3 | 2 |
| Wood | 2009-10-15 | 2009 | 10 | 15 |
| Brooke | 2014-09-24 | 2014 | 9 | 24 |
| Lake | 2018-01-01 | 2018 | 1 | 1 |
| Taylor | 2009-05-12 | 2009 | 5 | 12 |
| Brown | 2017-09-15 | 2017 | 9 | 15 |
| River | 2009-05-12 | 2009 | 5 | 12 |

Next, determine the difference in days between the current date and start_date with this:

```
SELECT lname, start_date,
       CURRENT_DATE  AS today,
       CURRENT_DATE - start_date AS diff
FROM employee
```

| lname | start_date | today | diff |
|-------|-----------|-------|------|
| Stream | 2020-03-02 | 2024-10-08 | 1681 |
| Wood | 2009-10-15 | 2024-10-08 | 5472 |
| Brooke | 2014-09-24 | 2024-10-08 | 3667 |
| Lake | 2018-01-01 | 2024-10-08 | 2472 |
| Taylor | 2009-05-12 | 2024-10-08 | 5628 |
| Brown | 2017-09-15 | 2024-10-08 | 2580 |
| River | 2009-05-12 | 2024-10-08 | 5628 |

*Dates in Hive*

In Hive, dates are given in the format yyyy-mm-dd:

```
SELECT lname, fname, start_date,
       DATE_FORMAT(start_date, 'dd.MM.yyyy') AS eur_date
FROM employee
WHERE start_date = '2009-05-12'
```

The column on the right will give you start_date as an example in European format.

Here is another example of extracting parts from dates:

```
SELECT lname, start_date,
       YEAR(start_date) AS yr,
       MONTH (start_date) AS mon,
       DAY(start_date) AS day
FROM employee
```

| LNAME | START_DATE | YR | MON | DAY |
|-------|------------|-----|-----|-----|
| Stream | 2020-03-02 | 2020 | 3 | 2 |
| Wood | 2009-10-15 | 2009 | 10 | 15 |
| Brooke | 2014-09-24 | 2014 | 9 | 24 |
| Lake | 2018-01-01 | 2018 | 1 | 1 |
| Taylor | 2009-05-12 | 2009 | 5 | 12 |
| Brown | 2017-09-15 | 2017 | 9 | 15 |
| River | 2009-05-12 | 2009 | 5 | 12 |

We calculate the number of days between the current date and start_date in employee:

```
SELECT lname, start_date,
FROM_UNIXTIME(UNIX_TIMESTAMP()) AS today,
  DATEDIFF(FROM_UNIXTIME(UNIX_TIMESTAMP()), start_date) AS diff
FROM employee
```

```
lname     start_date      today         diff
--------- ---------- ---------- ----------
Stream    2020-03-02 2024-10-08      1681
Wood      2009-10-15 2024-10-08      5472
Brooke    2014-09-24 2024-10-08      3667
Lake      2018-01-01 2024-10-08      2472
Taylor    2009-05-12 2024-10-08      5628
Brown     2017-09-15 2024-10-08      2580
River     2009-05-12 2024-10-08      5628
```

## *Dates in Snowflake*

In Snowflake, dates are given in the format yyyy-mm-dd:

```
SELECT lname, fname, start_date,
    TO_VARCHAR (start_date, 'dd.mm.yyyy') AS eur_date
FROM employee
WHERE start_date = '2009-05-12'
```

```
lname     fname       start_date                eur_date
------- ---------- ---------------------- -----------
Taylor    Peter       2009-05-12 00:00:00.000  12.05.2009
River     Lilian      2009-05-12 00:00:00.000  12.05.2009
```

The rightmost column will give the date in the European format. You can also use TO_CHAR.

Extracting the date parts:

```
SELECT lname, start_date,
YEAR(start_date) AS yr,
MONTH (start_date) AS mon,
DAY(start_date) AS day
FROM employee
```

```
LNAME     START_DATE                 YR    MON   DAY
-------   ----------------------     ----- ----  ---
Stream    2020-03-02 00:00:00.000    2020    3     2
Wood      2009-10-15 00:00:00.000    2009   10    15
Brooke    2014-09-24 00:00:00.000    2014    9    24
Lake      2018-01-01 00:00:00.000    2018    1     1
Taylor    2009-05-12 00:00:00.000    2009    5    12
Brown     2017-09-15 00:00:00.000    2017    9    15
River     2009-05-12 00:00:00.000    2009    5    12
```

Calculating the difference between the current date and start_date of employee:

```
SELECT lname, start_date, CURRENT_DATE AS today,
        DATEDIFF(day, start_date, CURRENT_DATE) AS diff
FROM employee
```

```
lname      start_date    today         diff
---------  ----------    ----------    ------
Stream     2020-03-02    2024-10-08    1681
Wood       2009-10-15    2024-10-08    5472
Brooke     2014-09-24    2024-10-08    3667
Lake       2018-01-01    2024-10-08    2472
Taylor     2009-05-12    2024-10-08    5628
Brown      2017-09-15    2024-10-08    2580
River      2009-05-12    2024-10-08    5628
```

## EXERCISES

1. Search for all employees who started working (start_date) later than 2017-09-14. Return empno, lname, fname, and start_date.

2. Extract the date parts of today: year, month and day (in numbers). In the result set, show these four columns: today, year, month, and day.

## 6.6 GROUPING

### GROUP BY

The GROUP BY clause groups the retrieved rows so that all rows in one group have the same value in the GROUP BY columns. The final result will have only one row per different values of the GROUP BY columns and usually one or more aggregate functions for the group (MIN, MAX, COUNT, SUM, or AVG). Let's take a look at an example:

*Calculate total hours per project.*

Here is the proj_emp table:

| PROJNO | EMPNO | HOURS_ACT | HOURS_EST |
| ------ | ----- | --------- | --------- |
| P1 | 2134 | 300 | 300 |
| P1 | 2245 | 200 | 300 |
| P1 | 3546 | 400 | 500 |
| P1 | 2884 | 100 | 200 |
| P1 | 2234 | 200 | NULL |
| P1 | 2345 | 100 | 100 |
| P1 | 3547 | 300 | 200 |
| P2 | 2134 | 300 | NULL |
| P2 | 2245 | 400 | 500 |
| P3 | 2245 | 900 | 100 |
| P4 | 2245 | 200 | 200 |
| P4 | 2234 | 300 | 400 |
| P4 | 2884 | 400 | 600 |

There are four projects: P1, P2, P3 and P4. The result should include the total hours for each project. The result set should have four rows, one for each project. This is done with GROUP BY:

```
SELECT projno, SUM(hours_act) AS hours_act_tot
 FROM proj_emp
 GROUP BY projno

PROJNO   HOURS_ACT_TOT
------   --------------
P1                1600
P2                 700
P3                 900
P4                 900
```

The GROUP BY clause is a little tricky. Take a careful look at the instructions below to get it right!

If the SELECT list contains both columns with aggregate functions (like SUM(hours_act)) and "normal columns" not involving aggregate functions, then ALL the "normal" columns of the SELECT list must be in the GROUP BY clause.

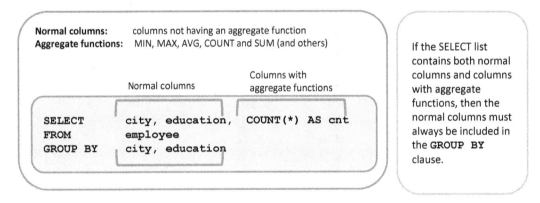

Figure 13: Get the count of employees per city and education.

```
SELECT city, education, COUNT(*) AS cnt
FROM employee
GROUP BY city, education

CITY          EDUCATION         CNT
----------    ----------    --------
LONDON        NULL               1
LONDON        PhD                1
LONDON        Ba                 1
SYDNEY        DIP                1
SYDNEY        Ba                 1
HELSINKI      MA                 2
```

The columns city and education are normal columns and COUNT(*) is an aggregate function. So both city and education must be listed in the GROUP BY clause (tip: cut and paste the list of all normal columns from the SELECT list to the GROUP BY list).

Here is a query with a column missing from the GROUP BY clause, an example of a typical mistake:

```
-- Error in this statement!
SELECT city, education, COUNT(*) AS cnt
FROM employee
GROUP BY city
```

This will result in an error message. You must add the column education to the GROUP BY list.

If a column in the GROUP BY clause contains several NULLs, they are grouped together as if they were of the same value!

Often, we use several aggregate functions in one query.

*Give us the minimum hours, maximum hours, and average hours for all projects except for project P2.*

```
SELECT projno, MIN(hours_act) AS minimum,
       MAX(hours_act) AS maximum,
       AVG(hours_act) AS average
 FROM proj_emp
 WHERE NOT projno = 'P2'
 GROUP BY projno
```

| PROJNO | MINIMUM | MAXIMUM | AVERAGE |
|--------|---------|---------|---------|
| P1     | 100     | 400     | 228     |
| P3     | 900     | 900     | 900     |
| P4     | 200     | 400     | 300     |

 Remember that you only need the GROUP BY clause if the SELECT list contains **both** "normal" columns **and** one or more aggregate functions (like MIN, MAX, COUNT, AVG or SUM). If this is not the case, you should not use GROUP BY.

## HAVING

The HAVING clause is not needed very often and you can skip this part on first reading. It comes in handy, for example, when searching for duplicate rows. See the chapter on searching for duplicate rows.

The result obtained using GROUP BY can be further narrowed down by using the HAVING clause. The HAVING clause has the same syntax as the WHERE clause, except that even aggregate functions are permitted. HAVING sets conditions on groups in the same way that WHERE sets conditions on rows.

*Which projects have at least three members? Show project number and employee count.*

Let's first take a look at all projects (we call this "the intermediate result").

```
SELECT projno, COUNT(*) AS cnt
FROM proj_emp
GROUP BY projno

PROJNO       cnt
------    -------
P1             7
P2             2
P3             1
P4             3
```

We want to restrict ourselves only to those projects where the row count (i.e., number of employees) is three or more in this intermediate result. We are not making a condition on a column of the table. Instead, we are using the aggregate function COUNT(*) to limit the groups to produce the final rows in the output. For that reason, we have to use the HAVING clause:

```
SELECT projno, COUNT(*) AS cnt
FROM proj_emp
GROUP BY projno
HAVING COUNT(*) >= 3

PROJNO       cnt
------    ------
P1             7
P4             3
```

When using **GROUP BY**, we can restrict the result in two ways:

- Restrict the rows that will be grouped in the first place, using the WHERE clause, as usual.

- After grouping, we have the intermediate result (groups). We then can use HAVING to further limit which groups are in the final result.

*Which projects have at least three employees with under 400 actual hours used for the project?*

```
SELECT projno
FROM proj_emp
WHERE hours_act < 400
GROUP BY projno
HAVING COUNT(*) >=3


PROJNO
----
P1
```

Before grouping, we discarded the rows where hours_act is 400 or more. After grouping, we excluded groups with fewer than three such employees. In the HAVING clause, you can use aggregate functions on any column of the table in the FROM clause, even if it is not in the SELECT list. You can also use subqueries (more details coming shortly).

*List the city and maximum salary for those cities where the maximum salary is less than the average salary of all employees (!).*

```
SELECT city, MAX(salary) AS max_salary
FROM employee
GROUP BY city
HAVING MAX(salary) <
          (SELECT AVG(salary)      -- this is a subquery
           FROM employee)


CITY         MAX_SALARY
----------   ----------
SYDNEY           2800
```

## EXERCISES

1. Calculate salaries by city (city and total salary for city). Order by city.

2. How many projects are there in each location? Get the location and amount (column heading cnt).

3. Which locations have at least two projects?

## 6.7 Calculation with Columns

As previously stated, we have after the word SELECT a list of columns or an asterisk (*), a shorthand for the list of all columns. The SELECT list can also contain calculations. In calculations, you can use functions, arithmetic operators, numeric constants, and columns from the tables. You can also do calculations in the WHERE clause as long as you don't use aggregate functions (like MIN, MAX, AVG, SUM, or COUNT).

*Calculate the tax paid using the salary and tax rate (tax percent). Fetch columns empno, lname, salary, tax_rate, and tax.*

```
SELECT empno, lname, salary,
       tax_rate, salary*tax_rate/100 AS tax
FROM employee
```

| EMPNO | LNAME | SALARY | TAX_RATE | TAX |
|-------|-------|--------|----------|-------|
| 2134 | Stream | 2800 | 22 | 616 |
| 2234 | Wood | 3100 | 33 | 1023 |
| 2245 | Brooke | 3100 | 31 | 961 |
| 2345 | Lake | 2800 | 24.5 | 686 |
| 2884 | Taylor | 2960 | 31 | 917.6 |
| 3546 | Brown | 2650 | 22 | 583 |
| 3547 | River | 2800 | 37 | 1036 |

The column "tax" in the result set is purely computational.

The alias name given to the calculated column (tax) cannot be further used in the SELECT clause or anywhere else in the SQL statement except for the ORDER BY clause (Snowflake is an exception to this rule). The following statement does not work, as logical as it might seem:

```
SELECT empno, lname, salary, tax_rate,
       salary*tax_rate/100 AS tax,
       salary - tax AS net    -- does not work!
FROM employee
```

You have to write the query this way:

```
SELECT empno, lname, salary, tax_rate,
       salary*tax_rate/100 AS tax,
       salary - salary*tax_rate/100 AS net
FROM employee
```

| EMPNO | LNAME | SALARY | TAX_RATE | TAX | NET |
|-------|-------|--------|----------|-----|-----|
| 2134 | Stream | 2800 | 22 | 616 | 2184 |
| 2234 | Wood | 3100 | 33 | 1023 | 2077 |
| 2245 | Brooke | 3100 | 31 | 961 | 2139 |
| 2345 | Lake | 2800 | 24.5 | 686 | 2114 |
| 2884 | Taylor | 2960 | 31 | 917.6 | 2042.4 |
| 3546 | Brown | 2650 | 22 | 583 | 2067 |
| 3547 | River | 2800 | 37 | 1036 | 1764 |

SQL can be used for quite complex calculations:

*What is the difference and percentage difference between planned hours (hours_est) and actual hours (hours_act)? Order by percentage difference.*

```
SELECT projno, empno, hours_act, hours_est,
    hours_act - hours_est AS  diff,
    100*(hours_est - hours_act)/hours_act  AS pros_diff
FROM proj_emp
ORDER BY pros_diff
```

| projno | empno | hours_act | hours_est | diff | pros_diff |
|--------|-------|-----------|-----------|------|-----------|
| P1 | 2234 | 200 | NULL | NULL | NULL |
| P2 | 2134 | 300 | NULL | NULL | NULL |
| P3 | 2245 | 900 | 100 | 100 | -50 |
| P1 | 2134 | 300 | 300 | 0 | 0 |
| P1 | 2345 | 100 | 100 | 0 | 0 |
| P4 | 2245 | 200 | 200 | 0 | 0 |
| P1 | 2983 | 400 | 500 | -100 | 25 |
| P2 | 2245 | 400 | 500 | -100 | 25 |
| P4 | 2234 | 300 | 400 | -100 | 33.3333 |
| P1 | 2245 | 200 | 300 | -100 | 50 |
| P4 | 2884 | 400 | 600 | -200 | 50 |
| P1 | 2884 | 100 | 200 | -100 | 100 |

ORDER BY pros_diff sorts the result according to the sixth, purely calculated column. We recommend giving all calculated columns a descriptive name and using this name in the ORDER BY clause. Some products sort NULLs at the end rather than at the beginning as above (which can be changed by putting NULL LAST or NULLS FIRST in the ORDER BY clause).

As we can see in the previous example, calculating with NULLs results in NULL. Something minus unknown is still unknown! However, often we want to treat NULLs as zero. We can do that with the special function COALESCE:

```
SELECT  projno, empno, hours_act,
        COALESCE (hours_est, 0) AS hours_est,
        hours_act - COALESCE (hours_est, 0)  AS diff,
    100*(COALESCE (hours_est, 0) - hours_act)/hours_act AS p_diff
FROM proj_emp
ORDER BY pros_diff
```

Now the result is different:

| projno | empno | hours_act | hours_est | diff | p_diff |
|--------|-------|-----------|-----------|------|--------|
| P1 | 2234 | 200 | 0 | 200 | -100 |
| P2 | 2134 | 300 | 0 | 300 | -100 |
| P3 | 2245 | 900 | 100 | 100 | -50 |
| P1 | 2134 | 300 | 300 | 0 | 0 |
| P1 | 2345 | 100 | 100 | 0 | 0 |
| P4 | 2245 | 200 | 200 | 0 | 0 |
| P1 | 2983 | 400 | 500 | -100 | 25 |
| P2 | 2245 | 400 | 500 | -100 | 25 |
| P4 | 2234 | 300 | 400 | -100 | 33.3333 |
| P1 | 2245 | 200 | 300 | -100 | 50 |
| P4 | 2884 | 400 | 600 | -200 | 50 |
| P1 | 2884 | 100 | 200 | -100 | 100 |

COALESCE will return zero if hours_est is NULL, otherwise it will return the value of hours_est.

Calculations are also allowed in the WHERE and HAVING clauses. Remember that in the WHERE clause, you can't use aggregate functions.

*Same as above, but return only the rows where the percentage difference is over 25 (now we don't care about NULLs):*

```
SELECT projno, empno, hours_act, hours_est,
       hours_act - hours_est   AS   diff,
       100*(hours_est - hours_act)/hours_act AS p_diff
FROM proj_emp
WHERE 100*(hours_est - hours_act)/hours_act > 25
ORDER BY perc_dif
```

| projno | empno | hours_act | hours_est | diff | p_diff |
|--------|-------|-----------|-----------|------|--------|
| P4 | 2234 | 300 | 400 | -100 | 33.3333 |
| P1 | 2245 | 200 | 300 | -100 | 50 |
| P4 | 2884 | 400 | 600 | -200 | 50 |
| P1 | 2884 | 100 | 200 | -100 | 100 |

Note that the percentage difference (p_diff) is now used in the SELECT list, as an ORDER BY value and even in the WHERE clause!

## EXERCISES

1. Calculate the tax using salary and tax rate. Return columns empno, lname, fname, salary, tax_rate, and tax. Order by the calculated tax from highest to lowest (descending order).

2. What is the difference between the minimum and maximum salary, and what percentage is the highest salary higher than the minimum salary? Include columns for minimum and maximum salary to help with checking.

3. Get the names and salaries of all employees whose salary would be more than 3000 with a 10% raise.

# CHAPTER SEVEN

# Joins

So far, we have selected data from only one table at a time. However, in well-designed realistic databases, the data is spread across several (normalized) tables and must be collected and combined to get the desired result set. This is done by using joins. Joins form a central part of SQL queries.

Tables can be joined using two different kinds of syntax. The newer and recommended one is the **join syntax** which we will introduce first. Then we describe the old syntax, the **traditional syntax**. Finally, we compare the two approaches.

## 7.1 Join Syntax

*Joining Two Tables*

The following figure demonstrates the idea of joining.

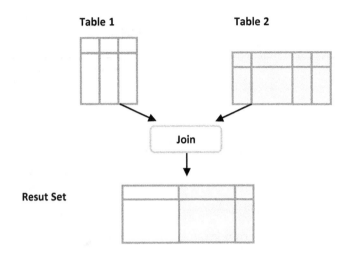

Figure 14: Joining combines columns from several tables into one result set.

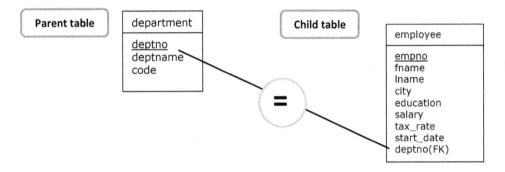

Figure 15: The table employee is the child table, whose foreign key (FK) deptno refers to the deptno column (PK) of the parent table (department). deptno values must be the same to "glue" the rows together into one row. This connection (the "join condition") is given in the ON clause: ON department.deptno = employee.deptno.

*Fetch all employees' names and departments that are from London. Order by department name.*

```
SELECT department.deptno, deptname, lname, fname, city
FROM department
    JOIN employee
    ON (department.deptno = employee.deptno) -- join condition
WHERE city = 'LONDON'
ORDER BY deptname
```

```
  DEPTNO  DEPTNAME     LNAME     FNAME    CITY
--------- ----------   -------   ------   -------
       1  IT           Wood      Mike     LONDON
       3  Production   Stream    Peter    LONDON
       3  Production   Lake      Leon     LONDON
```

We needed two tables to obtain the required data: department and employee. They are given in the FROM-part of the SELECT-statement. Now, all columns from both tables can be put in the SELECT list. It does not make any difference in which order you give the tables. Parenthesis in the ON -clause are only for clarity (not mandatory).

When joining rows from two tables, it is important to understand how the rows are combined. This information is given after the ON keyword of the FROM clause by describing which column (or columns) in the parent row must have the same value as the column (or columns) in the child row. If the corresponding columns have the same value in both rows, these rows are combined into a new row in the result set. In nearly all cases (but not always), we combine the primary key of the parent table (department.deptno) to the foreign key of the child table (employee.deptno). See Figure 16. On the left, we have the employee table with employees from London and on the right, we have the department table. The lines show how rows with the same deptno are combined.

Note that in this SQL example, the column name department.deptno refers to the column deptno in the department table. We say that we have **qualified** the deptno column when we prefix it with the name of the table it belongs to. Qualifying is necessary when a column of the same name can be found in two or more tables that take part in the join. In our example, there is a column named deptno in both tables department and employee.

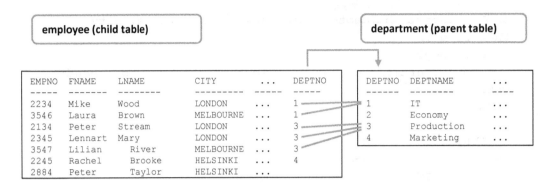

Figure 16: A concrete example of how rows are combined.

Without qualifying, the system would not know which column we are referring to and would protest with a nasty error message, usually containing the word "ambiguous". The columns empno, lname, fname, city, and deptname do not have to be qualified since columns with that name can only be found in one table.

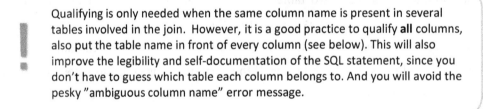

Qualifying is only needed when the same column name is present in several tables involved in the join. However, it is a good practice to qualify **all** columns, also put the table name in front of every column (see below). This will also improve the legibility and self-documentation of the SQL statement, since you don't have to guess which table each column belongs to. And you will avoid the pesky "ambiguous column name" error message.

This is how our new SQL statement looks like after applying the tip from above:

```
SELECT department.deptno, department.deptname,
       employee.lname, employee.fname, employee.city
FROM department
    JOIN employee
        ON (department.deptno = employee.deptno)
WHERE employee.city = 'LONDON'
ORDER BY department.deptname
```

From now on, we will always qualify column names in joins.

The columns used to join tables don't have to have the same name, but that is often the case in practice. They don't even have to have the same exact data type, but they must be similar enough (both character, numeric, etc.). For performance reasons, it is better to always have the exact same data type for corresponding parent-child columns. Data conversion might have a severe effect on performance if it inhibits the use of an index (see Chapter 22 Performance). You can add the keyword INNER before the JOIN keyword:

```
SELECT department.deptno, department.deptname,
       employee.lname, employee.fname, employee.city
  FROM department
     INNER JOIN employee
       ON (department.deptno = employee.deptno)
  WHERE employee.city = 'LONDON'
  ORDER BY department.deptname
```

This is effectively the same query as above. Because **INNER** is not mandatory, we don't use it in our examples.

## Correlation Names

We can give a table or a view a new name in the FROM clause. The new name is called the **correlation name**. Just add the correlation name after the original name, separated by a blank. Compare the previous example with the following one, where we are using the correlation names dep and emp for department and employee respectively:

```
SELECT d.deptno, d.deptname,
       e.lname, e.fname, e.city
FROM department d      -- correlation name for department is d
   JOIN employee e     -- correlation name for employee is e
     ON (d.deptno = e.deptno)
WHERE e.city = 'LONDON'
ORDER BY d.deptname
```

It is a good idea to use the correlation name instead of the table's actual name within the SQL statement. It is, of course, only used during the execution of the SQL statement and has no effect on the name of the table outside the statement. It is used in all parts of the SQL statement: SELECT list, WHERE clause, ORDER BY, etc. Correlation names come in handy, especially in joins, but they can be defined and used in any SQL SELECT statement. You are forced to use correlation names in self joins (when a table is joined to itself) and in some subqueries (see Chapter 9.2 Correlated Subqueries).

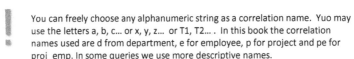

You can freely choose any alphanumeric string as a correlation name. Yuo may use the letters a, b, c... or x, y, z... or T1, T2... . In this book the correlation names used are d from department, e for employee, p for project and pe for proj_emp. In some queries we use more descriptive names.

When a correlation name is defined, the original table name cannot be used anymore for qualifying columns (in the same SQL statement). You **must** use correlation names everywhere. The following SQL statement would result in an error message:

```
SELECT department.deptno, department.deptname, employee.lname,
       employee.fname, employee.city    -- error!
FROM department d
     JOIN employee e                     -- correlation names d and e
        ON (d.deptno = e.deptno)
WHERE e.city = 'LONDON'
ORDER BY d.deptname
```

### Joining Several Tables

Joining is, of course, not restricted to two tables at a time. You can join as many tables as you want. Here is a three-table join. We need two join conditions:

*Fetch employee projects and hours using the names of employees and projects. Order by lname and project_name.*

First, using the original table names:

```
SELECT employee.empno, employee.lname, project.project_name,
proj_emp.hours_act
FROM employee
    JOIN proj_emp
       ON (employee.empno = proj_emp.empno)
    JOIN project
       ON (project.projno = proj_emp.projno)
ORDER BY employee.lname, project.project_name
```

| empno | lname | project_name | hours_act |
|-------|-------|--------------|-----------|
| 2245 | Brooke | ACCOUNTING | 200 |
| 2245 | Brooke | BILLING | 400 |
| 2245 | Brooke | BOOKKEEPING | 200 |
| 2245 | Brooke | WAREHOUSING | 900 |
| 3546 | Brown | BOOKKEEPING | 400 |
| 2345 | Lake | BOOKKEEPING | 100 |
| 3547 | River | BOOKKEEPING | 300 |
| 2134 | Stream | BILLING | 300 |
| 2134 | Stream | BOOKKEEPING | 300 |
| 2884 | Taylor | ACCOUNTING | 400 |
| 2884 | Taylor | BOOKKEEPING | 100 |
| 2234 | Wood | ACCOUNTING | 300 |
| 2234 | Wood | BOOKKEEPING | 200 |

Less typing is needed when using short correlation names:

```
SELECT e.empno, e.lname, p.project_name, pe.hours_act
FROM employee e
    JOIN proj_emp pe
       ON (e.empno = pe.empno)
    JOIN project p
       ON (p.projno = pe.projno)
ORDER BY e.lname, p.project_name
```

You can think of the previous SQL statement like this: First, join the employee table to the proj_emp table to create a temporary result set. To this result set, join the project table.

Which table is the project table related to? You can see that in the ON clause, ON (p.projno = pe.projno). That is, the proj_emp –table. And so on for more tables. Note that parenthesis are not required, they are there only for clarity.

Here is an example of a join with four tables:

```
SELECT d.deptname, e.empno, e.lname, p.project_name,
       p.projno, pe.hours_act
FROM department d
    JOIN employee e
      ON (d.deptno = e.deptno)
    JOIN proj_emp pe
      ON (e.empno = pe.empno)
    JOIN project p
      ON (p.projno = pe.projno)
ORDER BY d.deptname, e.lname
```

```
deptname    empno  lname         project_name  projno  hours_act
----------  -----  ------------  ------------  ------  ---------
IT          3546   Brown         BOOKKEEPING     P1    400
IT          2234   Wood          BOOKKEEPING     P1    200
IT          2234   Wood          ACCOUNTING      P4    300
Marketing   2245   Brooke        BOOKKEEPING     P1    200
Marketing   2245   Brooke        BILLING         P2    400
Marketing   2245   Brooke        WAREHOUSING     P3    900
Marketing   2245   Brooke        ACCOUNTING      P4    200
Research    2345   Lake          BOOKKEEPING     P1    100
Research    3547   River         BOOKKEEPING     P1    300
Research    2134   Stream        BOOKKEEPING     P1    300
Research    2134   Stream        BILLING         P2    300
```

An important rule is that each new table presented in the query must have a link to some previously mentioned table. The following query (the same as above, but table order is different) will produce an error, because the tables employee and project do not have any common columns.

```
SELECT d.deptname, e.empno, e.lname, p.project_name,
       p.projno, pe.hours_act
FROM department d
   JOIN employee e
     ON (d.deptno = e.deptno)
   JOIN project p
     ON (p.projno = pe.projno)   -- Error! unknown pe.projno
   JOIN proj_emp pe
     ON (e.empno = pe.empno)
ORDER BY d.deptname, e.lname
```

 Only mention the tables you really need in the query. All additional tables will potentially slow down your query.

### The ON clause

The ON clause is mainly used for join conditions, but you can add other conditions also:

```
SELECT d.deptno, d.deptname, e.lname, e.fname, e.city
FROM department d
   JOIN employee e
     ON (d.deptno = e.deptno
         AND e.city = 'LONDON')
  ORDER BY d.deptname
```

The result of this query is exactly the same as that of the other examples. One purpose of the Join syntax is to clarify the distinction between join conditions and other conditions by separating them into different parts of the SQL statement. However, the syntax above does not support this aim.

### EXERCISES

1. Get the projects of employee 2245. Return project name and actual hours worked on each project (you will need two tables: project and proj_emp).

Order by project_name. Empno is a character string, so remember to use quotes ('2245'). The result should look like this:

```
PROJECT_NAME        HOURS_ACT
----------------    ---------
ACCOUNTING                200
BILLING                   400
BOOKKEEPING               200
WAREHOUSING               900
```

2. Select project name, employee number, actual hours, and estimated hours for projects. Order by project name. Use tables project and proj_emp.

3. Find employees with a salary of 2800 or less. We need the following columns: deptname and depno from department and fname, lname, city, and salary from employee. Order by department name and employee last name.

4. Select project names, employee names, and actual hours per project for each employee (not totals). Which tables will you need to access? Order by project name and employee name.

---

## 7.2 "Traditional" Join Syntax

Up until now, we have been going through the Join syntax. There is also the older, original syntax, which we call the traditional join syntax. You are free to choose between either of these syntaxes, but we recommend using the Join syntax. We will go through the reasons in depth in Chapter 7.3 "The Advantages of the Join syntax". The queries below correspond to the queries made with the join syntax presented earlier.

An example of the traditional syntax:

```
SELECT d.deptno, d.deptname, e.lname, e.fname, e.city
FROM department d, employee e    -- comma-separated table names
WHERE d.deptno = e.deptno        -- join cond. in WHERE clause
AND e.city = 'LONDON'            -- search condition
ORDER BY d.deptname
```

The tables are given as a comma-separated list (in any order). The join condition is in the WHERE clause instead of the ON clause. If you need other search conditions, they are added to the WHERE clause and connected by the AND operator.

Here is an example of a join of several tables with the traditional syntax (corresponding to the query in the previous chapter):

```
SELECT e.empno, e.lname, p.project_name, pe.hours_act
FROM employee e, proj_emp pe, project p
WHERE e.empno = pe.empno          -- first join condition
AND p.projno = pe.projno          -- second join condition
ORDER BY e.lname, p.project_name
```

All tables are listed in the FROM clause. All join conditions are found in the WHERE clause. We have three tables, hence two join conditions.

Note also the example with four tables using the traditional syntax:

```
SELECT d.deptname, e.empno, e.lname, p.project_name,
       p.projno, pe.hours_act
FROM department d, employee e, proj_emp pe, project p
WHERE d.deptno = e.deptno
AND e.empno = pe.empno
AND p.projno = pe.projno
ORDER BY d.deptname, e.lname
```

## The Missing Join Condition

What happens if we accidentally leave out the join condition (WHERE d.deptno = e.deptno) from our first example?

```
SELECT d.deptno, d.deptname, e.lname, e.fname, e.city
FROM department d, employee e
WHERE e.city = 'LONDON'
ORDER BY d.deptname
```

| DEPTNO | DEPTNAME | LNAME | FNAME | CITY |
|--------|----------|--------|--------|--------|
| 4 | Marketing | Stream | Peter | LONDON |
| 4 | Marketing | Wood | Mike | LONDON |
| 4 | Marketing | Lake | Leon | LONDON |
| 2 | Economy | Stream | Peter | LONDON |
| 2 | Economy | Lake | Leon | LONDON |
| 2 | Economy | Wood | Mike | LONDON |
| 1 | IT | Stream | Peter | LONDON |
| 1 | IT | Lake | Leon | LONDON |
| 1 | IT | Wood | Mike | LONDON |
| 3 | Research | Stream | Peter | LONDON |
| 3 | Research | Lake | Leon | LONDON |
| 3 | Research | Wood | Mike | LONDON |

The result does not make any sense. It has 12 rows instead of the three rows of the correct answer. Let's take a closer look at the original tables: departments on the right and employees from London on the left:

| EMPNO | FNAME | LNAME | CITY | ... | DEPTNO | DEPTNO | DEPTNAME |
|-------|-------|-------|------|-----|--------|--------|----------|
| 2234 | Mike | Wood | LONDON | ... | 1 | 1 | IT |
| 2134 | Peter | Stream | LONDON | ... | 3 | 2 | Economy |
| 2345 | Leon | Lake | LONDON | ... | 3 | 3 | Research |
| | | | | | | 4 | Marketing |

Note that in our latest (incorrect!) join example, each department has been connected to **every** London employee. Three employees times four departments make 12 combinations, hence 12 rows. The purpose of the join condition is to tell the system to connect to department 1 only those employees with department number 1, etc. When the join condition is missing **all** rows from the first table, they are combined **with all rows** from the second table. That is, a cartesian product or cross join. Our database has very few rows, but imagine if one of the tables had 500,000 rows and the other one 1,000,000 rows. The result, without a join condition, would have 500,000 x 1,000,000 rows!

So, it is very important to always remember the join conditions. The missing join condition is the most common reason for a huge number of extra rows. Indeed, one of the advantages of our first join method, the Join syntax, is that we are forced to give the join condition and hence avoid the "cartesian product" problem.

In some rare cases, we actually need a cartesian product. Then, we use the CROSS JOIN. See Chapter 19.4.

## 7.3 The Advantages of the Join Syntax

Having acquainted ourselves with two methods for join, the traditional and the Join syntax, it is time to decide which one we should use. It is partly a matter of taste and habit, but we strongly recommend the Join syntax. Here are the reasons:

1. With the Join syntax, you will not forget the join condition because the ON clause is mandatory, and you will immediately get an error message if it is missing.

2. The Join syntax is clearer because the join conditions are separated from the normal conditions. With the traditional syntax, it is harder to distinguish between join conditions and other conditions, especially in more complex SQL statements with many tables and other conditions.

3. In any case, the Outer Join (see below) can only be done with the Join syntax. There are, however, some vendor-specific alternatives, such as (+) syntax in Oracle.

We will use the Join syntax in most of our examples. However, it is good to understand the traditional syntax, too, because you can still see it often in older programs and queries.

---

## 7.4 Outer Join

So far, we have been concerned only with "ordinary" joins (Inner Join). Next, we will look at another important type of join, the Outer Join.

*Select all projects and employees (empno and hours_act). Also include projects that do not involve employees ("childless fathers") in the result. Order by projno and empno.*

```
SELECT p.projno, p.project_name, pe.empno, pe.hours_act
FROM project p
     JOIN proj_emp pe
          ON (p.projno = pe.projno)
ORDER BY p.projno, pe.empno
```

| PROJNO | PROJECT_NAME | EMPNO | HOURS_ACT |
|--------|--------------|-------|-----------|
| P1 | BOOKKEEPING | 2134 | 300 |
| P1 | BOOKKEEPING | 2234 | 200 |
| P1 | BOOKKEEPING | 2245 | 200 |
| P1 | BOOKKEEPING | 2345 | 100 |
| P1 | BOOKKEEPING | 2884 | 100 |
| P1 | BOOKKEEPING | 3546 | 400 |
| P1 | BOOKKEEPING | 3547 | 300 |
| P2 | BILLING | 2134 | 300 |
| P2 | BILLING | 2245 | 400 |
| P3 | WAREHOUSING | 2245 | 900 |
| P4 | ACCOUNTING | 2234 | 300 |
| P4 | ACCOUNTING | 2245 | 200 |
| P4 | ACCOUNTING | 2884 | 400 |

**PROJECT**

| projno | project_name | priority | location |
|--------|--------------|----------|----------|
| P1 | BOOKKEEPING | 2 | LONDON |
| P2 | BILLING | 1 | HELSINKI |
| P3 | WAREHOUSING | 3 | HELSINKI |
| P4 | ACCOUNTING | 2 | LONDON |
| P5 | CUSTOMERS | 3 | SINGAPORE |
| P6 | STATISTICS | NULL | NULL |

**PROJ_EMP**

| projno | empno | hours_act | hours_est |
|--------|-------|-----------|-----------|
| P1 | 2134 | 300 | 300 |
| P1 | 2234 | 200 | NULL |
| P1 | 2245 | 200 | 300 |
| P1 | 2345 | 100 | 100 |
| P1 | 2884 | 100 | 200 |
| P1 | 3546 | 400 | 500 |
| P1 | 3547 | 300 | 200 |
| P2 | 2134 | 300 | NULL |
| P2 | 2245 | 400 | 500 |
| P3 | 2245 | 900 | 100 |
| P4 | 2884 | 400 | 600 |
| P4 | 2234 | 300 | 400 |
| P4 | 2245 | 200 | 200 |

**?**

Figure 17: There are no corresponding rows in table proj_emp for projects P5 and P6.

The result set is not correct, as there are no "empty" projects from the project table (P5 and P6). Empty projects do not have any employees. That is, rows in the proj_emp table. The inner join (or normal join) does not result in rows that don't have a corresponding row in the other table. For this, we need an **outer join,** which we do by just adding the keyword LEFT, as shown on the following page.

Now, the result set also includes rows for projects P5 and P6, as we had planned. For these rows, the empno and hours_act columns will be NULL (P5 and P6 don't have employees nor hours). With the normal inner join, the tables can be given in any order, but in an Outer Join, the order is important. The table on the left (the first table) is the one we want all rows from, even the rows that don't have "hits" (i.e., corresponding rows in the other table).

```
SELECT p.projno, p.project_name, pe.empno, pe.hours_act
FROM project p
LEFT JOIN proj_emp pe              -- Outer Join
    ON (p.projno = pe.projno)
ORDER BY p.projno, pe.empno
```

| PROJNO | PROJECT_NAME | EMPNO | HOURS_ACT |
|--------|--------------|-------|-----------|
| P1 | BOOKKEEPING | 2134 | 300 |
| P1 | BOOKKEEPING | 2234 | 200 |
| P1 | BOOKKEEPING | 2245 | 200 |
| P1 | BOOKKEEPING | 2345 | 100 |
| P1 | BOOKKEEPING | 2884 | 100 |
| P1 | BOOKKEEPING | 3546 | 400 |
| P1 | BOOKKEEPING | 3547 | 300 |
| P2 | BILLING | 2134 | 300 |
| P2 | BILLING | 2245 | 400 |
| P3 | WAREHOUSING | 2245 | 900 |
| P4 | ACCOUNTING | 2234 | 300 |
| P4 | ACCOUNTING | 2245 | 200 |
| P4 | ACCOUNTING | 2884 | 400 |
| P5 | CUSTOMERS | NULL | NULL |
| P6 | STATISTICS | NULL | NULL |

Optionally, you can add the keyword OUTER between LEFT and JOIN: LEFT OUTER JOIN. Because it is not mandatory, we leave it out. You can also use RIGHT JOIN. In this case, the main table (the one from which all rows are fetched) will be on the right side of the JOIN keyword.

This query brings the same result as the query above:

```
SELECT p.projno, p.project_name, pe.empno, pe.hours_act
FROM proj_emp pe
RIGHT JOIN project p              -- Outer Join
    ON (p.projno = pe.projno)
ORDER BY p.projno, pe.empno
```

It is also possible to specify an outer join in both directions by using FULL JOIN.

In legacy code, you might encounter product-specific outer join syntax. For instance, in Oracle, you can get the same result using the following SQL, traditional join syntax:

```
SELECT p.projno, p.project_name, pe.empno, pe.hours_act
FROM project p, proj_emp pe
WHERE p.projno = pe.projno(+)     - Oracle specific outer join
ORDER BY p.projno, pe.empno
```

Add (+) after the child table's foreign key in the join condition (i.e., the table that potentially will be unmatched). This syntax also works in Snowflake.

As mentioned earlier, we recommend using the Join syntax and also writing all outer joins with the Join syntax (also in Oracle and Snowflake).

>  Note. If you have an outer join with separate conditions on the child table you **must** read chapter "Outer Join – Advanced conditions" .

**EXERCISES**

1. Retrieve a list of departments and their employees. Columns deptno, deptname, fname and lname. Make sure all four departments are visible in the result regardless of whether they have employees. Order by deptno and lname.

2. Create a list of employees and their departments. Columns: lname, fname, deptno and deptname,. Make sure all employees are included regardless of whether they belong to a department. Order by lname and deptno.

## 7.5 Join and Group By Together

It is very common to have a query with both a join and group by. Note the columns in the GROUP BY clause: all non-aggregate columns from the SELECT list must be given.

*Retrieve department total salary and average salary by department.*

```
SELECT d.deptno, d.deptname,
SUM(e.salary) AS total,
       AVG(e.salary) AS average
FROM department d
LEFT JOIN employee e
    ON (d.deptno = e.deptno)
GROUP BY d.deptno, d.deptname
```

| DEPTNO | DEPTNAME | TOTAL | AVERAGE |
|--------|----------|-------|---------|
| 1 | IT | 5750 | 2875 |
| 2 | Economy | NULL | NULL |
| 3 | Research | 8400 | 2800 |
| 4 | Marketing | 3100 | 3100 |

### EXERCISES

1.  Select per employee the total of actual hours worked in all projects. We need the last name, firstname, the total hours worked (column heading hours_total), and the number of projects the employee is involved with (no_of_projects). GROUP BY and join needed. Order by lname and empno.

2.  Select per project (projno, project_name) the total actual hours (hours_act) and the difference between the actual hours and the estimated hours. Take only projects with a priority of 1 or 3. Do you have 2 or 3 rows in the result? Use appropriate column headings (alias names).

# CHAPTER EIGHT

# UNION

With UNION, you can combine one or more separate tables so that the result will consist of the union of the rows of these tables "on top of each other". The idea is to have two or more separate SELECT statements and combine them with the UNION clause. See Figure 18.

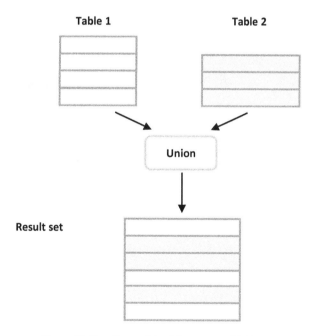

Figure 18: Results combined from several tables.

*Select all employees that have a salary over 2800 and/or belong to project P2. Order by lname.*

```
SELECT lname, '-salary  > 2800' AS type
 FROM employee
 WHERE salary > 2800
    UNION
 SELECT e.lname, 'works in project P2'
 FROM proj_emp pe
 JOIN employee e
     ON  (pe.empno = e.empno)
 WHERE pe.projno = 'P2'
 ORDER BY lname              -- order by involves the whole query


 LNAME     TYPE
 -------   --------------------
 Brooke    -salary  > 2800
 Brooke    works in project P2
 Stream    works in project P2
 Taylor    -salary  > 2800
 Wood      -salary  > 2800
```

The literal text in the SELECT list will appear on every row. The column names (headers) of the result set will be inherited from the first SELECT. You can use other names for columns in the remaining SELECT clauses (except for DB2 and Hive).

In our example, we have combined two SELECT statements, but there is no limit to the number of SELECT statements you can combine with UNION.

You must stick to the following rules when using UNION:

- All SELECT lists must have the same amount of columns and in the same order.

- The columns must be "union compatible" (they must be of the same data type or similar enough).

- There can be only one ORDER BY clause and it has to be at the very end.

- In the ORDER BY clause, you can either use the ordinal numbers of the columns which you want to order by or use the names of the columns from the first SELECT statement.

The UNION operation will eliminate duplicate rows from the result set (similar to DISTINCT). If you want to keep duplicate rows, use the UNION ALL format. UNION ALL is usually better in terms of performance (an internal sort is avoided). So, if you know that there are no duplicate rows in the entire UNION clause, use UNION ALL. This would be advisable also in our example above.

When using UNION, it is often necessary to change the name of the column using an alias name because the column name is always derived from the first SELECT. You can change the name of the column using "AS alias name" in the first SELECT of the UNION. Take a look at the previous example (and remember the separate rules for DB2 and Hive mentioned earlier).

UNION is very practical when combining several tables into the same structure. For instance, suppose we have active sales data in the table sales and the history in table saleshistory. With the following query, we get the rows from both tables in one query. Since SALES_DATE is included in the result, no duplicates can arise from combining the two tables, so we can use UNION ALL for performance reasons (the result will be the same as with UNION), as shown on the following page.

Or you might have monthly summary tables. Then you can build a query that combines all 12 months for a year. Write 12 SELECT queries (for each month) connected with UNION clauses. The query is very easy to use if you build a view on top of it (See Chapter 14 Views).

Chapter 17 concludes with another interesting example of UNION.

```
SELECT product_id, sales_date,
quantity_sold, sales_amount
FROM sales
WHERE prodgroup = 'ABC'
        UNION ALL        -- UNION without duplicate row elimination
SELECT product_id, sales_date,
quantity_sold, sales_amount
FROM saleshistory
WHERE prodgroup = 'ABC'
ORDER BY 1, 2           -- order by product_id, sales_date
```

## EXERCISES

1. We want all employees and projects in the same result set, which should be as below. For employees, city, and empno, and for projects, location, and projno. Each row should indicate whether it is an employee or a project (TYPE). Place the column headings (aliases) in the first SELECT. Sort by city from lowest to highest and by column ID from highest to lowest. (The NULL row can be at the beginning or end, depending on the database you are using.)

```
CITY            ID      TYPE
------------    ----    --------
HELSINKI        2884    EMPLOYEE
HELSINKI        2245    EMPLOYEE
HELSINKI        P3      PROJECT
HELSINKI        P2      PROJECT
LONDON          2345    EMPLOYEE
LONDON          2234    EMPLOYEE
LONDON          2134    EMPLOYEE
LONDON          P4      PROJECT
LONDON          P1      PROJECT
SYDNEY          3547    EMPLOYEE
SYDNEY          3546    EMPLOYEE
SINGAPORE       P5      PROJECT
NULL            P6      PROJECT
```

# CHAPTER NINE

# Subqueries

Subqueries allow you to restrict the rows of the main query using a nested query embedded in the main query. Queries can be nested several levels deep. This feature of SQL is what gave it the name (*Structured* Query Language). We will introduce the most common types of subqueries.

## 9.1 Basic Subqueries

### A Subquery that Returns One Row

Let's start with a simple example:

*Fetch all employees that live in the same city as the employee with the empno 2345 (Leon Lake). We will need the columns empno, lname, fname, and city.*

As a first step, let's find out which city employee '2345' lives in.

```
SELECT city
FROM employee
WHERE empno = '2345'

city
----------
LONDON
```

The city is London, so our next step is to retrieve all employees from London:

```
SELECT empno, lname, fname, city
FROM employee
WHERE city = 'LONDON'

EMPNO   LNAME     FNAME    CITY
-----   -------   ------   -------
2134    Stream    Peter    LONDON
2234    Wood      Mike     LONDON
2345    Lake      Leon     LONDON
```

We can combine the two queries, so we don't have to save the intermediate result (London) by hand or in a program variable. We use a subquery:

```
SELECT empno, lname, fname, city
FROM employee
WHERE city =
      (SELECT city
       FROM employee
       WHERE empno = '2345')

EMPNO   LNAME     FNAME    CITY
-----   -------   ------   -------
2134    Stream    Peter    LONDON
2234    Wood      Mike     LONDON
2345    Lake      Leon     LONDON
```

The execution of the query starts from the lowest subquery. First, the system executes the subquery to find the city of employee number 2345. **So, the execution order is bottom-**

**up.** The result is passed up to the next level and it is used to restrict the city of the main query.

The next query demonstrates a typical subquery. We will re-do a query we tried earlier, in Chapter 6.4 Functions, now using a subquery:

*Which employee(s) has the lowest tax rate?*

```
SELECT lname, fname, tax_rate
FROM employee
WHERE tax_rate =
  (SELECT MIN(tax_rate)      -- find the lowest tax rate
      FROM employee)


LNAME      FNAME    TAX_RATE
-------    ------   --------
Stream     Peter          22
Brown      Laura          22
```

The subquery first produces the lowest tax rate. Then, the main query gets all employees who have that tax rate.

## IN-Subqueries

Our subqueries have produced at most one row (or none) so far. It is common for a subquery to return more than one row. In such cases, we need to use the IN operator (also possible are ANY, SOME, or ALL). You can also use the EXISTS operator, which we will discuss shortly.

Let's see what happens if we use a subquery that returns several rows:

*Give the names of all employees from project P4.*

```
SELECT lname, fname
FROM employee
WHERE empno =
        (SELECT empno
         FROM proj_emp
         WHERE projno = 'P4')

   (SELECT empno
        *
ERROR:   single-row subquery returns more than one row
```

The system produces an error message, because the subquery returned more than one row (you might receive a different wording in your product). The subquery returns the set {'2245', '2234', '2884'} from the proj_emp table. You have to use the IN operator in cases where subqueries might return several rows:

```
SELECT lname, fname
FROM employee
WHERE empno IN
        (SELECT empno
         FROM proj_emp
         WHERE projno = 'P4')

LNAME       FNAME
---------   ----------
Wood        Mike
Brooke      Rachel
Taylor      Peter
```

The system executed the subquery first and returned a set of three empno values: {'2245', '2234', '2884'}. The main query returns the names of employees whose empno is in that set.

 First code the subquery and when it works build the main query on top of it. This way you can build your SQL statement step by step and test intermediate results after each step.

NOT IN is also often useful. You can express "not included in" queries with it:

*Which projects don't have any employees yet (or any more)?*

```
SELECT projno, project_name
FROM project
WHERE projno NOT IN
      (SELECT projno
       FROM proj_emp)


PROJNO   PROJECT_NAME
------   ---------------
P5       CUSTOMERS
P6       STATISTICS
```

The subquery produces an intermediate result that has all the projno values from the proj_emp table {'P1', 'P2', 'P3', 'P4'}. The main query will fetch all the projects that are NOT included in that list. Subqueries can be nested further within subqueries (except not in Hive, which supports only one level of subqueries):

*We want the names of all projects that have at least one employee with a salary of 2800.*

```
SELECT project_name
FROM project
WHERE projno IN
     (SELECT projno
      FROM proj_emp
      WHERE empno IN
         (SELECT empno
          FROM employee
          WHERE salary = 2800
          )
     )


PROJECT_NAME
---------------
BOOKKEEPING
BILLING
```

In the previous examples, we had only one column in the subquery, which was compared to one column in the higher level query (in the above query empno and projno). However, you can also compare a set of several columns (except for SQL Server and Hive, which allow only one column).

*Fetch employees from the table employee whose combination of first name and last name is found in the table employee2.*

```
SELECT *
FROM employee
WHERE (lname, fname) IN    -- not in SQL Server and Hive
    (SELECT lname, fname
     FROM employee2)
```

### EXERCISES

1. Search for all projects that have the same priority as project P5. Select the columns projno and project_name. Use a subquery.

2. Find the employees with the highest salary. Name and salary. There should be two employees.

3. Get the project names for employee 2134, using a subquery.

4. Get the employees (name) that are in at least one project with priority 1 or 3.

---

## 9.2 Correlated Subqueries – Connecting Subqueries to the Main Query

Correlated subqueries are not quite as common as uncorrelated ones (all subqueries until now in this chapter have been uncorrelated). You can skip this section if you wish, especially if you are new to subqueries.

The result of an uncorrelated subquery does not in any way depend on the main query. As we explained earlier, the system will first execute the subquery and then pass on the result to the containing query's WHERE clause. It would even be possible to execute the subquery separately (without parenthesis).

A *correlated subquery* is a subquery that uses column names from the main query. Hence, the subquery is connected or correlated, and cannot be executed independently. A column from a main query is referenced in the subquery and the subquery is executed separately for each row of the main query. So, the order of execution is now from top to bottom (top-down). This is how the system runs the query:

1.  Read the first row from the main query.
2.  For this row, execute the subquery using values from the row.
3.  Use the value of the subquery to determine if the row is selected or not.
4.  Read the next row from the main query, etc.

Let's take a look at a typical example of a correlated subquery.

*Who's salary is lower than the average salary of all employees in the same city?*

```
SELECT lname, fname, city, salary
FROM employee e1
WHERE  salary <
       (SELECT AVG(salary)
        FROM employee e2
        WHERE e2.city = e1.city)
```

| LNAME  | FNAME | CITY     | SALARY |
| ------ | ----- | -------- | ------ |
| Stream | Peter | LONDON   | 2800   |
| Lake   | Leon  | LONDON   | 2800   |
| Taylor | Peter | HELSINKI | 2960   |
| Brown  | Laura | SYDNEY   | 2650   |

The system reads the salary of the first employee. Then, it checks with a correlated subquery, whether the salary of this employee is less or equal to the average salary in his/her city. If it is, the row is selected; otherwise, it is discarded. Then, the system reads the next employee, does another subquery, etc. **The execution order is top-down**.

This is an example of a query where we need correlation names (e1 and e2) since both the main query and the subquery use the same table.

*Fetch top earners from each city. Order by city.*

```
SELECT city, salary, lname, fname
FROM employee e1
WHERE salary =
     (SELECT MAX(salary)
      FROM employee e2
      WHERE e2.city = e1.city)
ORDER BY city
```

| CITY | SALARY | LNAME | FNAME |
|------|--------|-------|-------|
| HELSINKI | 3100 | Brooke | Rachel |
| LONDON | 3100 | Wood | Mike |
| SYDNEY | 2800 | River | Lilian |

The two queries above represent correlated subqueries that can be very slow to execute. Some products (as for instance DB2) know how to save intermediate results so that the same value is not recalculated unnecessarily repeatedly. In other products you could use FROM + subquery + join or create a temporary table to join to.

**EXERCISES**

1. For each department (deptno), find the employee(s) with the earliest start_date. Return deptno, lname, fname, and start_date. Order by deptno.

## EXISTS

The EXISTS operator can be used to test the existence of rows of a certain value. An EXISTS subquery results in either true or false. So it does not return any other values (other then true or false) as in previous subqueries. EXISTS returns true if the subquery provides at least one row and false if no rows are found.

All IN subqueries can be converted into EXISTS or NOT EXISTS subqueries (this applies also to ALL and ANY queries). All EXISTS queries are, in practice, always correlated subqueries. That is, they refer to values in the main query. The execution order is from top to bottom.

Since the EXISTS subquery returns only values "true" or "false" to the main query, it does not make any difference what column names you use in the SELECT list of the subquery. You can just as well use SELECT *. Sometimes, you might see the form SELECT 1, which brings only the number one (which you never see), again because it has no effect what columns you use in the SELECT list.

*Get the numbers, names, and locations of projects that have employees connected to them.*

```
SELECT projno, project_name, location
FROM project p
WHERE EXISTS
      (SELECT *
       FROM proj_emp pe
       WHERE pe.projno = p.projno)

PROJNO   PROJECT_NAME   LOCATION
------   ------------   ----------
P1       BOOKKEEPING    LONDON
P2       BILLING        HELSINKI
P3       WAREHOUSING    HELSINKI
P4       ACCOUNTING     LONDON
```

First, the main query reads a row from the table project. Then, the subquery checks if at least one row exists in the proj_emp table for this project. If it does, the row (the columns projno, project_name, and location) from the project table is selected into the result set. Then the second row is read from the main query, and so on, until all rows in the project table have been checked.

*Which projects don't have any employees?*

```
SELECT projno, project_name
FROM project p
WHERE NOT EXISTS
       (SELECT *
        FROM proj_emp pe
        WHERE pe.projno = p.projno)

PROJNO PROJECT_NAME
------ ----------------
P5     CUSTOMERS
P6     STATISTICS
```

So P5 and P6 are the only projects that do not have any employees in the proj_emp table.

If you suspect that referential integrity has been compromised (see chapter 1.3 on integrity rules) you can find the orphan child rows with a query of the above type.

**EXERCISES**

1. Get the projects (project name) for employee 2245 using an EXISTS subquery.

2. List departments that do not have employees involved. Include department number and name.

# CHAPTER TEN

# Comparing Alternative Approaches

This chapter compares different SQL query approaches and gives recommendations.

## 10.1 Join or Subquery

By now, you probably understand that the same query can be written in many ways. The question arises of which one to choose. Here are some alternative ways to do the same query, each query returning the same result:

*Get the last name of the employees that belong to project P4.*

The first query on the following page is a subquery, the second one a join, and the third one a correlated subquery.

Query two, the join, has generally been considered the clearest. Query one, the subquery, takes second place among my students. What about performance? As long as the tables have appropriate indexes, the join (query 2) is potentially the most efficient. Option 1 may create an intermediate result table, after which the main query is executed. However, modern optimizers in many products can internally convert the subquery into a join. In any case, the best option is usually to **favor joins**.

```
1)  -- IN - subquery
    SELECT lname
    FROM employee
    WHERE empno IN
       (SELECT empno
        FROM proj_emp
        WHERE projno = 'P4')


LNAME
----------
Wood
Brooke
Taylor

2)   -- Join
     SELECT e.lname
     FROM employee e
     JOIN proj_emp pe
        ON e.empno = pe.empno
     WHERE pe.projno = 'P4'

3)   -- EXISTS - correlated subquery
     SELECT lname
     FROM employee e
     WHERE EXISTS
        (SELECT *
         FROM proj_emp pe
         WHERE projno = 'P4'
         AND pe.empno = e.empno)
```

Joins are easy to read and efficient. Do we actually need subqueries at all? Most subqueries can be converted into joins but not all. A subquery cannot be converted to a join in the following cases:

- The subquery has an aggregate function.
- The subquery is of the form NOT IN or NOT EXISTS.
- The subquery is in an UPDATE or DELETE statement.

Let's take a closer look at the subqueries and joins using the previous example:

*Get the last name of employees who belong to project P4.*

We present two methods to accomplish the task, IN subquery and join:

```
SELECT lname                    SELECT e.lname
FROM employee                   FROM employee e
WHERE empno IN                  JOIN proj_emp pe
    (SELECT empno                   ON e.empno = pe.empno
     FROM proj_emp              WHERE pe.projno = 'P4'
     WHERE projno = 'P4')


LNAME
----------

Wood
Brooke
Taylor
```

We now want to extend the result to include each employee's hours in project P4. In the join query, this is done like this:

```
SELECT e.lname, pe.hours_act
FROM employee e
    JOIN proj_emp pe
    ON e.empno = pe.empno
WHERE pe.projno = 'P4'

LNAME          HOURS_ACT
----------    ----------
Wood                 300
Brooke               200
Taylor               400
```

But in the subquery, we **cannot** show the hours column because the column is not present in the top-level query. Only the columns of the main query can be made available to the result set. The columns of the subqueries just control which rows are selected from the main query. Also, in this sense, a join is better than a subquery, because all columns from all tables in the FROM clause can be made visible (or copied to program variables in programs).

 The general rule is to use joins. In the case where you are only interested in the data from one table but want to use another table to restrict the rows (e.g. want only the customers that have orders) use an EXISTS or IN subquery. It is the most efficient method. If you want columns from several tables in the same result (e.g. customer data and order data on the same row) use join.

## 10.2 "Does not Belong" Type Queries

Previously, in Chapter 7, we demonstrated a query for projects without members. These kinds of queries are needed when we add a foreign key and want to ensure that there are no "orphan" rows in the child table. This query can be written in many ways.

*Show projects with no employees.*

With a NOT IN subquery, as shown on the facing page.

This kind of query is sometimes called Anti-Join or Set Difference.

Note that the NOT EXISTS query is generally more efficient than the IN-variant as long as we have a suitable index on the proj_emp table for the projno column. In our sample database, we have the index on columns (projno, empno), which works well with this query. Modern optimizers may end up with an equally efficient solution.

```
SELECT projno, project_name
 FROM project
 WHERE projno NOT IN
       (SELECT projno
        FROM proj_emp)


projno  project_name
------  ----------
P5      CUSTOMERS
P6      STATISTICS
```

Or with NOT EXISTS:

```
SELECT projno, project_name
 FROM project p
 WHERE NOT EXISTS
       (SELECT *
        FROM proj_emp pe
        WHERE pe.projno = p.projno)
```

EXCEPT is also possible:

```
SELECT projno
FROM project
EXCEPT        -- In Oracle use MINUS
SELECT projno
FROM proj_emp
```

Outer join works also well:

```
SELECT p.projno, p.project_name, pe.empno, pe.hours_act
FROM project p
   LEFT JOIN proj_emp pe
   ON p.projno = pe.projno
WHERE pe.empno IS NULL


projno  project_name  empno    hours_act
------  ------------  -----    ---------
P5      CUSTOMERS     NULL     NULL
P6      STATISTICS    NULL     NULL
```

The Left outer join generates NULL values to columns empno and hours_act for projects without employees. In the query, those NULL rows are selected. That is, the projects without employees.

**EXERCISES**

1.  List employees that do not have departments involved. Include the empno, lname and fname. Use LEFT JOIN.

---

## 10.3 Summary of the SELECT Statement

Here is a summary of the most important features of a SELECT statement in one query. The query itself does not make much sense, but it is a collection and repetition of key features.

*Select empno, lname, fname, tax_rate, and total hours_act for those employees that are from London or that have a salary more than 2800. In addition, these employees must have worked for over 500 hours on projects.*

```
SELECT e.empno, e.lname,          -- SELECT list "normal"
       e.fname, e.tax_rate,       -- columns
       SUM(p.hours_act) AS tot_hours  -- alias name tot_hours
FROM employee e
JOIN proj_emp pr                  -- correlation names to tables
        ON e.empno = p.empno      -- join condition
WHERE (city = 'LONDON'
        OR salary > 2800)         -- AND and OR: use parentheses
AND tax_rate =
    (SELECT MIN(tax_rate)         -- MIN function in subquery
      FROM employee)
GROUP BY e.empno, e.lname,        -- GROUP BY: list all "normal"
         e.fname, e.tax_rate      -- columns
HAVING SUM(p.hours_act) > 500
ORDER BY e.lname, tot_hours       -- ORDER BY at end
                                  -- Using alias name tot_hours


EMPNO LNAME        FNAME        TAX_RATE   TOT_HOURS
---- ----------   ----------   ----------  ----------
2134 Stream       Peter              22          600
```

## 10.4 Advice on How to Build a SELECT Statement

Here is some advice on how to approach the task of building a SELECT statement. Interestingly, the first part you should write is the FROM clause. Use the following order:

1. First, find out what columns you need for the result set.

2. Start from the FROM part:
   a. Examine what tables you need, to retrieve the columns in step 1.
   b. Write the FROM clause, use correlation names of you want to (e.g., FROM project p).
   c. If there is more than one table, combine them with JOIN.
   d. Write the ON condition (one or several of them).

3. Put the columns you want to get in the SELECT list (qualified by correlation names, if you used them).

4. Form the search criteria in the WHERE clause (if you are using both AND and OR, use parentheses).

5. If you need grouping, add the GROUP BY clause.

6. If you need sorting, add the ORDER BY clause (always at the very end).

It is worth proceeding step by step in complex queries, one table at a time, and testing in between. Remember to check after each stage that the result set is correct.

Don't add unnecessary tables to the query (tables whose columns you don't need or are not used to restrict data), or the query will slow down.

Don't select columns you don't need. Don't use "SELECT *" unless you just want to look at the table quickly. It may slow down your query. Selecting specific columns is also much more readable and easier to understand than "SELECT *". Someone can also change the structure of the table, e.g., add new columns. In this sense, "SELECT *" is unstable and to be avoided.

Format your SQL statements clearly on separate rows, as in examples in this book, not on a single line. Use correlation names for all columns in joins. Comment your SQL if it adds understanding.

## 10.5 Typical SELECT Statement Mistakes

If you make a syntax mistake, you get an error message and no result set. But if you make a logical mistake, you get a wrong result set. Here is a very useful list of typical logical mistakes:

1. Too many rows in the result

   a) Join condition missing in traditional join (see Chapter 7).

   b) Join condition has the same column two times, such as:

   ```
   SELECT d.deptno, d.deptname, e.lname,
          e.fname, e.city
   FROM department d
   JOIN employee e
       ON d.deptno = d.deptno     -- WRONG
   ```

   The ON -clause should be: `ON d.deptno = e.deptno`

   c) WHERE condition with AND and OR, but parentheses missing (see Page 56 Parentheses).

2. A correlated subquery misses rows that connect with a NULL

   a) One NULL does not equal another NULL (NULL = NULL is not true), for instance

   ```
   WHERE e1.deptno = e2.deptno
   ```

Instead use this, it converts NULLs to zeros so that we get the desired result:

```
WHERE COALESCE(e1.deptno, 0)  = COALESCE(e2.deptno, 0)
```

Here zero is used. Choose another value (e.g., 10), if zero appears as a value in that column.

3. Rows where NULLs don't appear even if we were searching for them

    a) We used the form = NULL (like WHERE location = NULL).

        ⇨   use IS NULL ( WHERE location IS NULL).

4. Too many rows in a GROUP BY query

    a) Make sure that GROUP BY list does not include extra columns, other than the "ordinary columns" in the SELECT list. (See 6.6 Grouping).

5. Same value for an aggregate function (sum, average, etc.) appears on each row when using GROUP BY in a join

    a) Join condition missing; this results in a all-to-all join and the sum will be the same for each row. (See mistakes 1a and 1b above).

6. Missing rows in a negation query (NOT or <>)

    a) NULLS are not included. Add a NULL condition or use COALESCE. Such as:

```
SELECT *
FROM project
WHERE priority <> 2
OR priority IS NULL
```

Without the NULL condition, rows with priority NULL are not included.

7. Missing rows in JOIN

a) Inner join is used and rows are missing from the result. Try outer join (e.g., LEFT JOIN or RIGHT JOIN).

8. Missing rows in OUTER JOIN (LEFT JOIN, RIGHT JOIN or FULL JOIN)

a) Search conditions on the child table must be made part of the ON condition or use a subquery as a table.

(See Chapter 19.3)

9. The rows are in the wrong order

a) ORDER BY is missing. Remember that GROUP BY does not guarantee that the rows will be in the order of the columns in GROUP BY. Only ORDER BY guarantees the correct order of rows.

10. Wrong header in the result set and column missing from the result set

a) The comma was missed in the SELECT list. See example below. What is supposed to be a column is taken as a column alias name (no AS word). Check the columns, add missing commas and use the AS word for column alias names.

```
SELECT project_name location
FROM project
```

Comma missing: location will erroneously be the column name for column project_name.

As you see in the list above, you might get a nice-looking result set, which is wrong. Tip: for a new query, check that the result set is right.

# CHAPTER ELEVEN

# Table Definitions

We will first deal with the creation and altering of tables.

## 11.1 Creating Tables Introduction

The creator of the table must have the appropriate authority. A table is created in an existing database. When you create a table, you define the name of the table and the columns that belong to it. For each column, you define:

- The name of the column

- The data type (e.g., numeric)

- For some column types, the maximum length and possible decimals of a decimal number

- Other possible constraints and clauses:
    - NOT NULL; NULL is not allowed. By default, NULL is allowed
    - CHECK clause for limiting the set of allowed values
    - DEFAULT clause for default value

   ○ UNIQUE clause to indicate that the column has to be unique on every
     row

   ○ PRIMARY KEY and FOREIGN KEY clauses for primary and foreign
     keys (I will deal with these later)

Let's take a look at a small example that works in all of the book's products:

```
CREATE TABLE department
(deptno    SMALLINT  NOT NULL  PRIMARY KEY,
deptname    VARCHAR(50),
code     VARCHAR(30))
```

The name of the table is department. The columns are deptno, deptname, and code. The deptno column is defined as mandatory (NOT NULL) and also as the table's primary key. In most products, the primary key definition includes the mandatory feature. It has the data type SMALLINT, which means a small integer (in Oracle, it corresponds to NUMBER). The column deptname is a variable-length character string with a maximum length of 50 characters. When you create the table, your database management product will save all the information of the table (table name, column names, etc.) in its system catalog.

According to Codd's relational model, all tables must have a primary key definition which is a great guide also in practice. However, database products do not require a PRIMARY KEY clause, so a table can be created without one. Sometimes, you might use temporary or work tables that don't need a primary key. In the mainframe version of DB2, a unique index must be created for the primary key. In other products, this is done automatically. In Snowflake and Hive, the primary key definitions have no effect.

In many products, various physical configurations can also be defined when creating tables, such as which physical disk area, table space, or segment the table is created in and how much space is allocated to the table and how it is extended. In general, these configurations can be omitted, and they are automated. For critical databases, it is advisable to consult our local database administrator.

In MySQL, you must decide whether to use regular tables or InnoDB tables. InnoDB tables support referential integrity and transaction processing. Add TYPE=InnoDB at the end of the create table statement.

---

## 11.2 Data Types

All products have the datatype CHAR[**(length)**]. It is fixed length, which means that all columns always take up the same amount of space. Let's take a look at the following example:

```
deptno CHAR(15)
```

Even if the department ID is only one character, the space used is always 15 characters. If, on the other hand, the data type VARCHAR[(length)] (e.g., VARCHAR(50)) is used, the space will adjust itself to the true length of the value. Longer columns should favor this format. Here are some of the most common data types by product. See your manual for a complete list.

**Oracle data types:**

```
CHAR [(length)]         fixed length character string, default
                        length 1, maximum 2000
VARCHAR2[(length)]      variable length character string, max
                        4000 characters
LONG                    variable length strings up to 2 G
NUMBER [(length[,desim.part])]   suitable for most numeric
                                 columns
DATE                    date and time
BLOB                    binary large object, max 4 G
BIT                     one bit
```

The most used data types in Oracle are VARCHAR2, NUMBER, and DATE.

**SQL Server data types:**

```
CHAR [(length)]              fixed length character string,
                             default length 1, maximum 8000
VARCHAR[(length)]            variable length character string,
max 8000
TEXT                         variable length strings up to 4 G
MONEY, SMALLMONEY            suitable for currencies
INT                          integer, -2^32 - 2^31-1, takes four
                             bytes
SMALLINT                     integer, -2^15 - 2^15-1,
                             takes two bytes
TINYINT                      0 - 255
BIGINT                       integer, -2^63 - 2^63-1, takes
                             eight bytes
DECIMAL [(length[,desim.part])]  a fixed precision number,
                             e.g. DECIMAL (5,2) means that
                             the length of the entire
                             number is five digits, two of
                             which are decimal digits
FLOAT                        floating point number
DATE                         date value between 0001-01-01 and
                             9999-12-31
DATETIME                     date and time covering 1753-01-01
                             to 9999-12-31 with 0,003 sec
                             precision
DATETIME2                    date and time covering 0001-01-01
                             to 9999-12-31 with nanosec
                             precision
```

## DB2 data types:

| | |
|---|---|
| CHAR [(length)] | fixed length character string, default length 1, maximum 254 |
| VARCHAR[(length)] | variable length character string, max 32672 |
| CLOB | variable length strings up to 2 G |
| BLOB | binary large object, max 2 G |
| INT | integer, $-2^{32} - 2^{31}-1$, takes four bytes |
| SMALLINT | integer, $-2^{15} - 2^{15}-1$, takes two bytes |
| BIGINT | integer, $-2^{63} - 2^{63}-1$, takes eight bytes |
| DECIMAL [(length[,desim.part])] | fixed precision number, e.g. DECIMAL (5,2) means that the length of the entire number is five digits, two of which are decimal digits |
| FLOAT | float |
| DATE | date between 0001-01-01 and 9999-12-31 |
| TIME | time value: hours, minutes seconds |
| TIMESTAMP | date and time, up to nanosecond resolution |

## MySQL data types:

| | |
|---|---|
| CHAR [(length)] | fixed length character string, default length 1 |
| VARCHAR[(length)] | variable length character string, max 8000 characters |
| INT | integer, n. -2000 milj. - 2000 milj |
| SMALLINT | integer, -32768 - 32767 |
| MEDIUMINT | integer, about -8 milj - 8 milj with sign |
| BIGINT | large integer, ca. 19 digits |
| DECIMAL [(length[,desim.part])] | fixed precision number, saved as a string |
| FLOAT | floating point number |
| DATE | date between 1000-9999 |
| DATETIME | date and time |

## PostgreSQL data types:

| | |
|---|---|
| CHAR [(length)] | fixed length character string |
| VARCHAR[(length)] | variable length character string |
| TEXT | variable length character string max 2G |
| INTEGER | integer, $-2^{32}$ - $2^{31}-1$, takes four bytes |
| SMALLINT | integer, $-2^{15}$ - $2^{15}-1$, takes two bytes |
| BIGINT | integer, $-2^{63}$ - $2^{63}-1$, takes eight bytes |
| DECIMAL [(length[,desim.part])] | a fixed precision number, e.g. DECIMAL (5,2) means that the length of the entire number is five digits, two of which are decimal digits |
| NUMERIC | a fixed precision number |
| SERIAL | auto incrementing integer |
| DATE | date |
| TIMESTAMP | date and time, microsecond resolution |

## Hive data types:

```
CHAR [(length)]        fixed length character string
VARCHAR[(length)]      variable length character string
STRING                 character string
INTEGER                integer, -2^32 - 2^31-1, takes four bytes
SMALLINT               integer, -2^15 - 2^15-1, takes two bytes
BIGINT                 integer, -2^63 - 2^63-1, takes eight
                       bytes
DECIMAL [(length[,desim.part])]   a fixed precision number,
                                  e.g. DECIMAL (5,2) means that
                                  the length of the entire
                                  number            is five
                                  digits, two of which are
                                  decimal digits
FLOAT                  floating point number
SERIAL                 auto incrementing integer
DATE                   date
TIMESTAMP              date and time, microsecond resolution
```

## Snowflake data types:

```
VARCHAR[(length)]      variable length character string, max and
default ca. 16 milj. chars
CHAR [(length)]        as previous but default is VARCHAR(1)
STRING                       same as VARCHAR
NUMBER [(length[,desim.part])]   fixed numeric, default (38,0)
INT, SMALLINT, BIGINT integer data types
DECIMAL                a fixed precision number
FLOAT                  floating point
DATE                   date
TIMESTAMP              date and time, see manual for other
                       TIMESTAMP variations
```

## 11.3 Creating Tables

Let's create the employee table in the simplest format, without referential integrity (referential integrity will be discussed in the next chapter). The database diagram and column descriptions can be found in Chapter 4.2, Figure 9.

```
CREATE TABLE employee
(empno      CHAR (4) PRIMARY KEY,   -- for DB2 add NOT NULL
 fname      VARCHAR (40),           -- In Oracle use VARCHAR2
 lname      VARCHAR (40),
 city       VARCHAR (40),
 education  CHAR (8),
 salary     DECIMAL(8, 2),
 tax_rate   DECIMAL(3,1),
 start_date DATE,
 deptno     SMALLINT)               -- In Oracle use NUMBER
```

The primary key cannot be NULL. Most products will automatically add the NOT NULL definition, so it suffices to specify PRIMARY KEY. In DB2, NOT NULL has to be specified, otherwise you will get an error message.

 As a rule, as many columns as possible should be defined as mandatory (NOT NULL) and specify a default value. You will avoid awkward NULL problems

### *Create a Table by Copying*

We often want to create a table with the same structure as an existing table. This can be done, see below. However, note that neither the primary key and foreign key definitions nor the CONSTRAINT definitions (except NOT NULL) are copied to the new table.

Here's how to create a new table with the same structure as the project table.

Snowflake and DB2:

```
CREATE TABLE proj1 LIKE project
```

Oracle, PostgreSQL, Hive, Snowflake and MySQL:

```
CREATE TABLE proj1 AS
SELECT *
FROM project
WHERE 1 = 2
```

Since 1 is not 2 (usually:), no rows are copied, but the table is created.

SQL Server and PostgreSQL:

```
SELECT * INTO proj1
FROM project
WHERE 1 = 2
```

If you want to copy a table with rows, just leave out the WHERE clause.


## Referential Integrity

Referential integrity rules can be defined for tables. It is not mandatory, but good in terms of integrity. The use of referential integrity is decided during database design. If you want the database management system to maintain referential integrity, you should provide the definitions. As a Data warehouse product, Snowflake does not force referential integrity rules, but you can define them for documentation reasons. The same applies to Hive.

Next, we create the table proj_emp with referential integrity defined and rules for situations where rows are deleted from the parent table (the next chapter will discuss the situation where the primary key is updated).

Oracle, DB2, SQL Server, PostgreSQL, Snowflake (in Snowflake and Hive only informational):

```
CREATE TABLE proj_emp
(projno         CHAR (4)  NOT NULL,
 empno          CHAR (4)  NOT NULL,
 hours_act         SMALLINT,              --in Oracle, use NUMBER(6)
 hours_est SMALLINT,
 CONSTRAINT proj_emp_pk  PRIMARY KEY (projno, empno),
 CONSTRAINT proj_emp_employee FOREIGN KEY (empno)
                REFERENCES employee (empno),
 CONSTRAINT proj_emp_project FOREIGN KEY (projno)
                REFERENCES project (projno)
                ON DELETE CASCADE);
```

In MySQL we are using the InnoDB table type, where referential integrity is supported. The parent tables employee and project must also be of InnoDB type.

```
CREATE TABLE proj_emp
(projno CHAR (4)   NOT NULL,
 empno    CHAR (4)   NOT NULL,
 hours_act SMALLINT,
 hours_est SMALLINT,
 INDEX(empno),
 INDEX(projno),
 CONSTRAINT proj_emp_pk PRIMARY KEY (projno, empno),
 CONSTRAINT proj_emp_employee FOREIGN KEY (empno)
     REFERENCES employee (empno),
 CONSTRAINT proj_emp_project FOREIGN KEY (projno)
     REFERENCES project (projno)
     ON DELETE CASCADE)
 TYPE = InnoDB;
```

The FOREIGN KEY definitions above prevent referential integrity violations for all products as follows:

- You can't delete rows from the employee table that have rows associated with them in the child table proj_emp.

- When you delete a row from the project table, then the child rows of it are automatically deleted from the table proj_emp. That is, a cascading delete takes place.
- You cannot add a row to the proj_emp table if the parent row is missing from either the employee table or the project table.
- The empno column cannot be modified in the employee table and the projno column cannot be modified in the project table if there are corresponding child rows in the proj_emp table.
- You cannot change the empno column in the proj_emp table to a non-existing value in the parent table employee column empno.
- You cannot change the deptno column in the proj_emp table to a non-existing value in the parent table department column deptno.

Let's try to remove, for example, employee 2134, Peter Stream, who as we well know, has projects in the proj_emp table.

In Oracle:

```
DELETE FROM employee
WHERE empno = '2134';

ERROR on row 1:
ORA-02292: integrity constraint (TEST.PROJ_EMP_EMPLOYEE)
violated - child record found
```

Oracle gave an error message, the delete failed. SQL Server has this to say:

```
DELETE statement conflicted with COLUMN REFERENCE constraint
'proj_emp_employee'. The conflict occurred in database 'test',
table 'proj_emp', column 'empno'.
The statement has been terminated.
```

MySQL error message looks like this:

```
ERROR 1217: Cannot delete or update a parent row: a foreign key
constraint fails
```

Next, let's see how the cascading delete from the project table works. First, a quick look at the current content of the project and proj_emp tables:

```
SELECT *
FROM project
```

| PROJNO | PROJECT_NAME | PRIORITY | LOCATION |
|--------|--------------|----------|-----------|
| P1 | BOOKKEEPING | 2 | LONDON |
| P2 | BILLING | 1 | HELSINKI |
| P3 | WAREHOUSING | 3 | HELSINKI |
| P4 | ACCOUNTING | 2 | LONDON |
| P5 | CUSTOMERS | 3 | SINGAPORE |
| P6 | STATISTICS | | |

```
SELECT *
FROM proj_emp
```

| PROJNO | EMPNO | HOURS_ACT | HOURS_EST |
|--------|-------|-----------|-----------|
| P1 | 2134 | 300 | 300 |
| P1 | 2245 | 200 | 300 |
| P1 | 3546 | 400 | 500 |
| P1 | 2884 | 100 | 200 |
| P1 | 2234 | 200 | NULL |
| P1 | 2345 | 100 | 100 |
| P1 | 3547 | 300 | 200 |
| P2 | 2134 | 300 | NULL |
| P2 | 2245 | 400 | 500 |
| P3 | 2245 | 200 | 100 |
| P4 | 2245 | 200 | 200 |
| P4 | 2234 | 300 | 400 |
| P4 | 2884 | 400 | 600 |

Let's remove P2 from the project table:

```
DELETE FROM project
WHERE projno = 'P2'
```

P2 was deleted from the project table; because of the DELETE CASCADE rule, the two P2-rows from the proj_emp table also disappeared!

```
SELECT *
FROM project
```

| PROJNO | PROJECT_NAME | PRIORITY | LOCATION |
|--------|--------------|----------|----------|
| P1 | BOOKKEEPING | 2 | LONDON |
| P3 | WAREHOUSING | 3 | HELSINKI |
| P4 | ACCOUNTING | 2 | LONDON |
| P5 | CUSTOMERS | 3 | SINGAPORE |
| P6 | STATISTICS | NULL | NULL |

```
SELECT *
FROM proj_emp
```

| PROJNO | EMPNO | HOURS_ACT | HOURS_EST |
|--------|-------|-----------|-----------|
| P1 | 2134 | 300 | 300 |
| P1 | 2245 | 200 | 300 |
| P1 | 3546 | 400 | 500 |
| P1 | 2884 | 100 | 200 |
| P1 | 2234 | 200 | NULL |
| P1 | 2345 | 100 | 100 |
| P1 | 3547 | 300 | 200 |
| P3 | 2245 | 200 | 100 |
| P4 | 2245 | 200 | 200 |
| P4 | 2234 | 300 | 400 |
| P4 | 2884 | 400 | 600 |

Next, we redefine the employee table with referential integrity. In Oracle, DB2, SQL Server, PostgreSQL, and MySQL we add a FOREIGN KEY definition that if you delete a department that has employees in the employee table, those department number references

(FK) will be set to NULL. So a department can be removed, and at the same time, the employees of the department are marked "orphan", not belonging to any department.

Oracle:

```
CREATE TABLE employee (
empno     CHAR (4) PRIMARY KEY,
fname     VARCHAR2 (40),
lname     VARCHAR2 (40),
city      VARCHAR2 (40),
education CHAR (8),
salary    DECIMAL(7, 2),
tax_rate DECIMAL(3,1),
start_date      DATE,
deptno    NUMBER (6),
CONSTRAINT fk_emp_dep FOREIGN KEY (deptno)
         REFERENCES department(deptno)
         ON DELETE SET NULL)
```

DB2, PostgreSQL:

```
CREATE TABLE employee (
empno     CHAR (4) PRIMARY KEY NOT NULL,
fname     VARCHAR (40),
lname     VARCHAR (40),
city      VARCHAR (40),
education CHAR (8),
salary    DECIMAL(7, 2),
tax_rate DECIMAL(3,1),
start_date      DATE,
deptno    SMALLINT,
CONSTRAINT fk_emp_dep FOREIGN KEY (deptno)
         REFERENCES department(deptno)
         ON DELETE SET NULL)
```

MySQL:

```
CREATE TABLE employee (
empno      CHAR (4) PRIMARY KEY,
fname     VARCHAR(40) ,
lname     VARCHAR(40) ,
city    VARCHAR(40) ,
education CHAR (8) ,
salary    DECIMAL(7, 2) ,
tax_rate DECIMAL(3,1) ,
start_date        DATETIME,
deptno     SMALLINT,
INDEX (deptno),
CONSTRAINT fk_emp_dep FOREIGN KEY (deptno)
          REFERENCES department(deptno)
          ON DELETE SET NULL)
TYPE = InnoDB;
```

SQL Server:

```
CREATE TABLE employee (
empno      CHAR (4) PRIMARY KEY,
fname     VARCHAR (40),
lname     VARCHAR (40),
city    VARCHAR (40),
education CHAR (8),
salary    DECIMAL(7, 2),
tax_rate DECIMAL(3,1),
start_date        DATETIME,
deptno     SMALLINT
CONSTRAINT fk_emp_dep FOREIGN KEY (deptno)
          REFERENCES department(deptno)
          ON DELETE SET NULL)
```

*Referential Integrity Update Rules*

In addition to deletion rules, there are rules for cascading the update of a parent table's primary key to the child table. The example does not work in DB2 (and, obviously, not in Hive and Snowflake).

```
CONSTRAINT proj_emp_employee FOREIGN KEY (empno)
    REFERENCES employee (empno),
    ON UPDATE CASCADE
```

Now, if the employee number changes, the change will be cascaded to the proj_emp table. However, it would be better to design the primary key so that it cannot change.

*Check Constraints and Default Values*

Check constraints can be defined at the table level to prevent incorrect information from entering the database. They are especially convenient if data is entered directly into the table manually or via some tool. However, checking the data entered with applications should be programmed in the user interface to give an error message about the incorrect data immediately after entering the data.

Table-level integrity checks, on the other hand, only take place when all the data has been received and the entire row is added to the table, which is too late. If the integrity rules are already encoded in the user interface, adding them to the database level a second time might feel unnecessary. However, if very high integrity is desired, this can be done.

Check constraints for data to be entered or updated can be performed with the CHECK clause. Here are some examples:

```
CREATE TABLE employee_test
(empno   CHAR (4)   NOT NULL
    CONSTRAINT empno_tark
      CHECK (empno BETWEEN '1000' AND  '9999'),
lname  VARCHAR (10) NOT NULL,
city  VARCHAR (10),
education CHAR(8)
   CONSTRAINT edu_check NOT NULL
     CHECK (education IN ('Ba', 'PhD', 'MA', 'DIP')) )
```

We insert a wrong value into the column education:

```
INSERT INTO employee_test
    VALUES ('6546', 'Smith','Liverpool', 'MB');


ERROR on row 1:
ORA-02290: check constraint (TEST.EDU_CHECK) violated
```

The DEFAULT clause can be used to specify a default value that will be given to the column if no value is given in the insert statement (otherwise, the column would be NULL). You can also set it to be the current user (USER) or current date or timestamp (CURRENT_DATE). In this example, the priority will be set to 2 if it is not given:

```
priority SMALLINT DEFAULT 2
```

In DB2, you can specify NOT NULL WITH DEFAULT. It allows the column value to be missing on insert and will set default values as follows: numbers will be zero, character strings blank, and dates will default to the current date. The UNIQUE attribute prevents duplicate values in the column. For instance, we don't want two projects to have the same name:

```
CREATE TABLE project
(projno   CHAR (4)   NOT NULL,
 project_name  CHAR (40) UNIQUE,
 <etc...>
```

You can also specify it in the form UNIQUE(project_name), so that there can be more than one column in the parentheses. UNIQUE allows for one NULL. Usually, products automatically create a unique index to enforce the UNIQUE clause.

## 11.4 Auto Increment Primary Key

Often, simple integers are used as primary keys (instead of natural keys). They convey no meaning, and they are called surrogates. They make updating actual natural keys easier since they are now not scattered all over the database. Surrogates are common in operational systems and in data warehousing star schema implementations.

All products in this book have the ability to automatically generate surrogate values by giving the next number. An automatically generated surrogate does not always guarantee that there are no gaps (in some situations, a value might go unused), but they are well-suited in most cases.

You can create a special sequencing object in Oracle, Snowflake, and DB2 to obtain the next integer.

```
CREATE SEQUENCE dept_no START WITH 1 INCREMENT BY 1
```

The starting value and increment of 1 are defaults, so they can be omitted. This is how to use the sequence:

```
INSERT INTO DEPARTMENT (deptno, deptname, code)
            VALUES(dept_no.NEXTVAL,'IT','asa_123456');
INSERT INTO DEPARTMENT (deptno, deptname, code)
            VALUES(dept_no.NEXTVAL,'Economy','s''dfg*234');
SELECT * FROM department;


    DEPTNO  DEPTNAME  CODE
 ---------- --------  ------------------------------
         1  IT        asa_123456
         2  Economy   s'dfg*234
```

The current value of the sequence can be obtained as follows (not in Snowflake):

```
SELECT dept_no.CURRVAL
FROM dual;


    CURRVAL
 ----------
          2
```

In DB2 the sequence is created similarly:

```
CREATE SEQUENCE department_nro START WITH 1 INCREMENT BY 1;
INSERT INTO DEPARTMENT (deptno, deptname, code)
    VALUES(NEXTVAL FOR department_nro,'IT','asa_123456');
INSERT  INTO DEPARTMENT  (deptno, deptname, code)
    VALUES(NEXTVAL FOR department_nro,'Economy','s''dfg*234');
SELECT * FROM department;


    DEPTNO  DEPTNAME  CODE
 ---------- --------  ------------------------------
         1  IT        asa_123456
         2  Economy   s'dfg*234
```

In DB2 the other alternative is to use a so-called IDENTITY column.

```
CREATE TABLE DEPARTMENT
(
deptno    SMALLINT    NOT NULL
          GENERATED ALWAYS AS IDENTITY
          (START WITH 1, INCREMENT BY 1),
deptname  VARCHAR(15),
code    VARCHAR(30)  ,
CONSTRAINT department_pk PRIMARY KEY(deptno)
);
INSERT INTO DEPARTMENT (deptname, code)
                  VALUES('IT','asa_123456');
INSERT  INTO DEPARTMENT  ( deptname, code)
                  VALUES('Economy','s''dfg*234');
SELECT * FROM department;


  DEPTNO  DEPTNAME   CODE
----------  --------   ------------------------------
      1  IT          asa_123456
      2  Economy     s'dfg*234
```

SQL Server and Snowflake have a similar IDENTITY column definition:

```
CREATE TABLE DEPARTMENT(
deptno    SMALLINT  NOT NULL IDENTITY (1, 1),
deptname  VARCHAR(15),
code    varCHAR(30)  ,
CONSTRAINT department_pk PRIMARY KEY(deptno));
INSERT INTO DEPARTMENT (deptname, code)
              VALUES('IT','asa_123456');
INSERT  INTO DEPARTMENT  ( deptname, code)
                VALUES('Economy','s''dfg*234');
SELECT * FROM department;


  DEPTNO  DEPTNAME   CODE
----------  --------   -------------------------------
      1  IT          asa_123456
      2  Economy     s'dfg*234
```

MySQL uses the following syntax:

```
CREATE TABLE DEPARTMENT(
deptno    SMALLINT AUTO_INCREMENT NOT NULL,
deptname  VARCHAR(15),
code    varCHAR(30)  ,
CONSTRAINT department_pk PRIMARY KEY(deptno));
INSERT INTO DEPARTMENT (deptname, code)
                  VALUES('IT','asa_123456');
INSERT  INTO DEPARTMENT  ( deptname, code)
                  VALUES('Economy','s''dfg*234');
SELECT * FROM department;

    DEPTNO  DEPTNAME    CODE
  ----------  ---------  -------------------------------
          1  IT          asa_123456
          2  Economy     s'dfg*234
```

In PostgreSQL:

```
CREATE TABLE department (
deptno    SERIAL NOT NULL,
deptname  VARCHAR(15),
code    VARCHAR(30),
CONSTRAINT department_pk PRIMARY KEY(deptno));
```

---

## 11.5 Altering Tables

*Adding a Column*

In SQL, it is very easy to add new columns to existing tables, even if they are already filled with data. We add the new column "type" to the project table.

```
ALTER TABLE project
    ADD type VARCHAR (20)
```

The new column goes to the end of the table. If you define the new column as NOT NULL (not allowing NULLs), you have to provide a default value, which will be given to the new column for all the existing rows.

## Modifying and Dropping a Column

The ALTER statement can be used to increase the length of a column. You can even change the data type if the table is empty. Let's increase the length of "type" to twenty (it is now 20 characters).

SQL Server:

```
ALTER TABLE project
    ALTER COLUMN type VARCHAR(40)
```

Oracle:

```
ALTER TABLE project
    MODIFY type VARCHAR2(40)
```

Snowflake and MySQL:

```
ALTER TABLE project
    MODIFY type VARCHAR(40)
```

DB2:

```
ALTER TABLE project
    ALTER COLUMN type SET DATA TYPE VARCHAR(40)
```

PostgreSQL:

```
ALTER TABLE project
    ALTER COLUMN type TYPE VARCHAR(40)
```

Hive:

```
ALTER TABLE project
    CHANGE type VARCHAR(40)
```

A column can be dropped like this:

```
ALTER TABLE project
    DROP COLUMN type
```

## Adding and Removing Foreign and Primary Keys

Referential integrity rules and primary keys can be added and removed from existing tables with the ALTER TABLE statement. In fact, it is common to first create the tables and then add the primary and foreign keys separately. It is a good idea to give constraints a name. This way, you can easily remove it later and the system will not generate cryptic names for the constraints. Let's drop the referential integrity definition from proj_emp that has to do with the employee table. Then we add it back, remove it, and add a primary key to proj_emp.

```
ALTER TABLE proj_emp
    DROP CONSTRAINT proj_emp_employee
ALTER TABLE proj_emp
ADD CONSTRAINT proj_emp_employee FOREIGN KEY (empno)
    REFERENCES employee(empno)
ALTER TABLE proj_emp
    DROP CONSTRAINT proj_emp_pk
ALTER TABLE proj_emp
    ADD CONSTRAINT proj_emp_pk PRIMARY KEY (projno, empno)
```

These statements work in all products in this book except for Hive and Snowflake, which don't support referential integrity.

---

## 11.6 Name Changes

You might need to change table and column names from time to time. Below are some examples that should be self-explanatory. Changing the name of the table will invalidate views built on the table in most products. Not all name changes are possible, for instance, if there are references from other tables.

DB2, MySQL:

```
RENAME TABLE project_log TO log    -- table name change
ALTER TABLE log RENAME COLUMN location TO city   -- column name
                                                 -- change
```

Oracle:

```
RENAME project_log TO log    -- table name change
ALTER TABLE log RENAME COLUMN location TO city   -- column name
                                                 -- change
```

SQL Server:

```
sp_rename 'project_log', 'log'     -- table name change
sp_rename 'log.location', 'city'   -- column name change
```

PostgreSQL:

```
ALTER TABLE project_log TO log       -- table name change
ALTER TABLE log RENAME COLUMN location TO city   -- column name
                                                 -- change
```

Hive:

```
ALTER TABLE project_log RENAME TO log      -- table name change
ALTER TABLE log CHANGE location city VARCHAR(15)  -- column
                                           -- name change
```

Snowflake:

```
ALTER TABLE project_log RENAME TO log      -- table name change
ALTER TABLE log RENAME COLUMN location TO city  -- column name
                                           -- change
```

## 11.7 Temporary Tables

Often, we need temporary, short-term tables to save intermediate results, especially in procedures and triggers. The content of the temporary table will disappear as soon as the session with the database is closed.

A temporary table in Oracle:

```
CREATE GLOBAL TEMPORARY TABLE w_project
(projno   CHAR(4) PRIMARY KEY,
 project_name  VARCHAR2(40),
 priority   NUMBER(2),
 location   VARCHAR2(15))
ON COMMIT PRESERVE ROWS;
```

The table exists permanently, but the content is different for each user session and will be emptied at the end of the session. The table can be used to pass data between transactions. The clause ON COMMIT DELETE ROWS (the default) will result in the rows being deleted at COMMIT. This will improve performance since no logging is needed for the temporary data.

In PostgreSQL and Snowflake, set up a temporary table like this:

```
CREATE GLOBAL TEMPORARY TABLE w_project
(projno   CHAR(4) PRIMARY KEY,
 project_name   VARCHAR2(40),
 priority     NUMBER(2),
 location   VARCHAR2(15))
```

The table will be automatically dropped after the session or transaction.

DB2 has its own syntax for temporary tables. To create the table, you first have to create a so-called table space for it, a file in the file system:

```
CREATE USER TEMPORARY TABLESPACE temppi
MANAGED BY SYSTEM USING ('C:\temp\temptable');
DECLARE GLOBAL TEMPORARY TABLE w_project
(projno   CHAR(4),
 project_name   VARCHAR(40),
 priority     SMALLINT,
 location   VARCHAR(15))
   IN temptable;
```

The owner of the table will be SESSION. Let's insert our projects into the temporary table:

```
INSERT INTO SESSION.W_PROJECT
SELECT *
FROM project
```

When the user ends the session, the table and rows will disappear.

In SQL Server, the temporary tables are created in the same way as permanent tables but with the name prefixed with # in the case of local temporary tables and ## with global temporary tables. The tables are created in the tempdb database. The data in the local temporary table is visible only in the session in which it was created. The global one is visible to all users and will disappear when everybody who is referring to the table has dropped their session.

```
CREATE TABLE #w_project        -- local temporary table
(projno  CHAR(4) PRIMARY KEY,
 project_name  VARCHAR(40),
 priority    SMALLINT,
 location  VARCHAR(15))
```

In SQL Server, you can also create a third kind of temporary table: the table variable. A table variable is only alive during the execution of a batch. That is, a set of statements executed between GOs. Otherwise, a table variable behaves as a temporary table. For performance reasons, it is advisable to use table variables for small numbers of rows only and, in general, rather use local temporary tables.

```
DECLARE @w_project TABLE
(projno  CHAR(4) PRIMARY KEY,
 project_name  VARCHAR(40),
 priority    SMALLINT,
 location  VARCHAR(15))
```

 A user might need an intermediate table, but we are hesitant to grant him the authority to create tables because of company policy or other reasons. The creation of temporary tables does not need separate authority, so it solves this problem.

## 11.8 Dropping Tables

You need to have the proper authority to drop tables. Be very careful: dropping a table will also erase all data (rows) that was in the table!

For example:

```
DROP TABLE employee
```

You can't drop a table if there exist other tables with FOREIGN KEY references to that table. You first have to drop the FOREIGN KEY.

There might be indexes, views and synonyms defined on the table. In most SQL products, those objects will also be removed if the base table is dropped. In Oracle and SQL Server, the views will remain but will be marked as invalid.

In Snowflake, there is a handy statement that recovers a dropped table!

```
UNDROP TABLE employee
```

## EXERCISES

1. Create a new table proj_hours with the columns projno, project_name, and hours_sum (hours_sum is of data type INTEGER). Look up the datatypes from figure 9 in Chapter 4. Set projno as the primary key. Test a SELECT * to the table, it shows column names (of course, no rows yet). In Oracle test with DESC.

2. Add the column priority to the new proj_hours table, datatype SMALLINT. Test again with SELECT *, in Oracle DESC.

3. Change the name of column hours_sum to hours_total.

# CHAPTER TWELVE

# Maintaining Table Data

In this chapter, we introduce the operations for adding, updating, and deleting table rows. All these statements apply also to views, if the views are among those that can be updated. See the chapter on views for more information on view updating. To run these commands, you need to be given the appropriate authority.

## 12.1 Adding Rows to a Table

*Adding One Row*

To add one row to a table, simply use an INSERT statement and give all values for the row. In the following example, one row is added to the department table, giving the values to the columns deptno, deptname, and code:

```
INSERT INTO department
VALUES (5, 'Purchase', 'asd')
```

The names of the receiving columns can (and should!) be given in parenthesis after the name of the table. This must always be done when all columns are not given a value (values only for a part of columns).

```
INSERT INTO department (deptno, deptname)
VALUES (6, 'Sales')
```

Let's take a look at what the table looks like after adding these two rows:

```
SELECT *
FROM department
ORDER BY deptno
```

```
    DEPTNO  DEPTNAME    CODE
---------- ---------   -------------
         1  IT          asa_123456
         2  Economy     s'dfg*234
         3  Research    a_ss*8888
         4  Marketing   a%
         5  Purchase    asd
         6  Sales       NULL
```

A NULL was generated for the code column for department 6 because the column was not included in the column list. The column in question must allow for NULLS. That is, it cannot be defined with the NOT NULL specification.

The same result can be obtained using the keyword NULL:

```
INSERT INTO department (deptno, deptname, code)
VALUES (6, 'Sales', NULL)
```

Strong recommendation:
Always use the INSERT INTO department (depno, depname, code) –type format, i.e. list all columns receiving a value in the column list after the table name. This will ensure that your query still works even if new columns are added to the table. It is also more descriptive from a documentation perspective.

*Adding Several Rows*

The following statement is an actual super statement, maybe the most powerful in SQL!

The INSERT SELECT statement is very useful in situations where data has to be summed, refined, or formatted and inserted into another table, which is typical in data warehouse processes. The result of a SELECT query is inserted directly into the table. It also has very good performance because everything happens inside the database.

We have a table busy_project, which has the exact same format as the project table. At the beginning, it is empty.

*Copy all rows with the value of priority 1 or 2 from project to busy_project.*

```
INSERT INTO busy_project
        (projno, project_name, priority, location)
SELECT projno, project_name, priority, location
FROM project
WHERE priority IN (1, 2)
```

Three rows were inserted into busy_project.

```
SELECT *
FROM busy_project
```

| PROJNO | PROJECT_NAME | PRIORITY | LOCATION |
| ------ | ------------ | -------- | -------- |
| P1 | BOOKKEEPING | 2 | LONDON |
| P2 | BILLING | 1 | HELSINKI |
| P4 | ACCOUNTING | 2 | LONDON |

The table in the SELECT statement can be the same one as the table in the target table of the insert statement.

Note that because the formats of the two tables are identical, we could have given the INSERT statement without listing the columns:

```
INSERT INTO busy_project        -- Dangerous statement!
SELECT *
FROM project
WHERE priority IN (1, 2)
```

Never use this kind of INSERT statement in programs or procedures! It is like a ticking time bomb: if a new column is ever added to the project table, (which is quite simple by using the ALTER TABLE statement), the statement will fail the next time it is executed because the receiving table busy_project will lack receiving columns. Instead, list the columns in both the subquery and the receiving table, like in the example we first introduced. As a bonus, the statement will be more self-documenting.

Let's continue with one more example. We have created a table called londoners with the columns empno, lname, fname, added_timestamp, and added_user.

*Copy the London employees from the employee table to the londoners table (3 employees). Add the current date and current user to the corresponding columns.*

```
INSERT INTO londoners
        (empno, lname, fname, timestamp , user )
SELECT empno, lname, fname, CURRENT_DATE, USER
FROM employee
WHERE city = 'LONDON'
```

The function CURRENT_DATE returns the current date. In Hive, use CFROM_INIXTIME(UNIX_TIMESTAMP()). Many Oracle users are used to SYSDATE, and SQL Server users use GETDATE(). The function USER returns the id of the logged in user (this does not work in Hive). See the query on the facing page.

```
SELECT *
  FROM londoners

empno   lname     fname  timestamp                user
-----   --------  -----  -----------------------  ----
2134    Stream    Peter  2024-10-13 18:43:41.357  Ari
2234    Wood      Mike   2024-10-13 18:43:41.357  Ari
2345    Lake      Leon   2024-10-13 18:43:41.357  Ari
```

Now we can see who has inserted rows and when.

In data warehouse environments, we often create summary tables which are much faster to use than queries on the original tables and are also easier to use. For example, sales transactions are often aggregated at the daily and/or monthly levels.

Let's simulate the case by adding rows to the employee_total summary table with the following columns: first name, last name, salary, and a sum of all the hours from all his/her projects.

*Add names, salaries, and project hour summaries to the summary table employee_total.*

```
INSERT INTO employee_total (lname, fname, salary, total)
SELECT e.lname, e.fname, e.salary, SUM(pe.hours_act)
FROM employee e
    JOIN proj_emp pe
    ON e.empno = pe.empno
GROUP BY e.lname, e.fname, e.salary
```

It is now fast and easy to query the summary table. Here is the result:

```
SELECT *
  FROM employee_total
```

| LNAME  | FNAME  | SALARY | TOTAL |
|--------|--------|--------|-------|
| Brooke | Rachel | 3100   | 1000  |
| Lake   | Leon   | 2800   | 100   |
| Taylor | Peter  | 2960   | 500   |
| Wood   | Mike   | 3100   | 500   |
| Brown  | Laura  | 2650   | 400   |
| Stream | Peter  | 2800   | 600   |
| River  | Lilian | 2800   | 300   |

Of course, the summary table needs to be refreshed from time to time.

**EXERCISES**

1.  Add a new project P7 to your own project table (project5, for example). The name is APOLLO and the location is NEW YORK. The priority is unknown. Remember to use quotes.

2.  Retrieve project number, project name, priority and sum of hours and insert the result set into your new table proj_hours (which has columns projno, project_name, hours_total, priority). You need a join between the project and proj_emp tables, as well as grouping. Helpful tip: create the SELECT first, and once it works, add the INSERT statement above.

## 12.2 Update

As an example of a one-row update, we will change the priority and location of project P2. Note that when updating more than one column at a time, the columns are separated by a comma.

*Change priority and location of project P3 to 2 and PARIS, respectively.*

```
UPDATE project
SET priority = 2,
    location = 'PARIS'
WHERE projno = 'P3'
```

The content of the project table is now the following:

```
projno  project_name   priority  location
------  -------------  --------  ----------
P1      BOOKKEEPING    2         LONDON
P2      BILLING        1         HELSINKI
P3      WAREHOUSING    2         PARIS
P4      ACCOUNTING     2         LONDON
P5      CUSTOMERS      3         SINGAPORE
P6      STATISTICS     NULL      NULL
```

Next, we will look at a set level update. This is very powerful but be careful!

*Give a 10% raise to all employees from HELSINKI. Employees from other cities do not need a raise :-)*

```
UPDATE employee
SET salary = salary * 1.1
WHERE city = 'HELSINKI'
```

Two rows were updated.

```
SELECT lname, fname, city, salary
FROM employee

LNAME           FNAME      CITY         SALARY
---------       -------    ---------    ------
Stream          Peter      LONDON         2800
Wood            Mike       LONDON         3100
Brooke          Rachel     HELSINKI       3410
Lake            Leon       LONDON         2800
Taylor          Peter      HELSINKI       3256
Brown           Laura      SYDNEY         2650
River           Lilian     SYDNEY         2800
```

*The project hours for P2 have been incorrectly reported. Clear the current hours. We will use the NULL keyword.*

```
UPDATE proj_emp
SET hours_act = NULL
WHERE projno = 'P2'
```

Two rows were updated.

*The workload of all department 3 employees must be reduced by 10%. Update the hours_est value for those employees.*

```
UPDATE proj_emp
   SET  hours_est = hours_est * 0.9
WHERE empno IN
   (SELECT empno FROM employee
    WHERE deptno = 3)
```

Four rows were updated.

```
SELECT *
  FROM proj_emp

PROJNO  EMPNO  HOURS_ACT  HOURS_EST
------  -----  ---------- ----------
P1      2134         300        270
P1      2245         200        300
P1      3546         400        500
P1      2884         100        200
P1      2234         200        NULL
P1      2345         100         90
P1      3547         300        180
P2      2134         300        NULL
P2      2245         400        500
P3      2245         900        100
P4      2245         200        200
P4      2234         300        400
P4      2884         400        600
```

The previous update used a subquery. The same table that is being updated can also be queried in a subquery.

The SQL update and delete statements are very powerful and it is easy to make some big mistakes. If you are updating the database online (using interactive SQL), we recommend using a two-step approach. This will give you more confidence and lessen the possibility of errors:

1. Use a SELECT statement and fetch the rows you want to update by using the exact same WHERE condition as in the update statement you are planning to run. You can now verify that the rows you have just fetched are the correct ones. That is, the ones you want to update. If the table is very large you can use COUNT(*) to see how many rows would qualify for the update or delete. From this, you can deduce whether the number of rows seems correct.

2. Create the UPDATE or DELETE statement using the exact same WHERE clause as in step 1. You can now be confident that the update or delete will target the intended rows.

If you are unsure of the update, it might be a good idea to make a backup of the table if it is not too large. You can do this by making a copy of the table with rows (Chapter 11.3).

 If you want to update several columns of a table it is faster to update them all at once using one SQL statement, instead of each column with a separate SQL statement.

**EXERCISES**

1. Change the name of department 1 ('IT') to 'IT Management'.

2. Add one to all priorities of projects in London (priority = priority + 1).

---

## 12.3 Delete

You can delete one row from a table by using the primary key (or another unique column).

*Delete the employee with the empno 2986.*

```
DELETE FROM employee
WHERE empno = '2986'
```

If you try removing a row from a parent table with related rows in a child table and the referential integrity relationship has been defined in the database, you will get an error message. However, if the referential integrity rule has been defined with the cascade rule (ON DELETE CASCADE ) the delete will "cascade" to the child rows, and they will also be deleted automatically. See Chapter 11 on referential integrity.

You can delete several rows at once. This is a powerful set level operation.

*Remove all employees for project P4 from the proj_emp table.*

```
DELETE FROM proj_emp
WHERE projno = 'P4'
```

Three rows were deleted from the proj_emp table.

Now let's look at a more complex example:

*Remove projects from the project table that don't have any employees associated with them.*

First, we'll list the current content:

```
SELECT *
FROM project

projno   project_name   priority   location
------   ------------   --------   ----------
P1       BOOKKEEPING           2   LONDON
P2       BILLING               1   HELSINKI
P3       WAREHOUSING           3   HELSINKI
P4       ACCOUNTING            2   LONDON
P5       CUSTOMERS             3   SINGAPORE
P6       STATISTICS         NULL   NULL
```

Then, we will remove projects with no employees:

```
DELETE FROM project          or      DELETE FROM project
WHERE projno NOT IN                  WHERE NOT EXISTS
    (SELECT projno                       (SELECT *
     FROM proj_emp)                       FROM proj_emp
                                          WHERE proj_emp.projno
                                                  = project.projno)
```

Two rows were deleted.

```
SELECT *
FROM project

projno  project_name  priority   location
------  ------------  ---------  ----------
P1      BOOKKEEPING          2   LONDON
P2      BILLING              1   HELSINKI
P3      WAREHOUSING          3   HELSINKI
P4      ACCOUNTING           2   LONDON
```

Watch out for the following, innocent looking example:

```
DELETE FROM proj_emp
```

All rows were deleted!

Emptying a large table using DELETE is slow because the system maintains a log of the deleted rows in case the command must be roll backed. For instance, in the case of a power failure. You might have tables containing temporary data (intermediate results, etc.) that need to be emptied from time to time. For that you can use the fast TRUNCATE TABLE command that is available in most of the products.

```
TRUNCATE TABLE proj_emp
```

Note that you can't reverse the deletion using ROLLBACK. Truncate can't be used on a table that has child tables, and it does not activate triggers that might be associated to the table. In SQL Server, TRUNCATE TABLE resets the IDENTITY counter (see Chapter 11.4 on identity columns).

**EXERCISES**

1.  Remove project P2 from your new table proj_hours.

# CHAPTER THIRTEEN

# Transaction Management

Transaction management is a central part of most database management products. In this chapter, we will briefly cover the basics of transactions.

## 13.1 What is a Transaction?

A transaction is a set of SQL statements (INSERT, UPDATE, DELETE) that are either all carried out in their entirety, or none of them are executed. In our example, we have an "account withdrawal" transaction where we withdraw n dollars from account t. The transaction consists of two steps:

```
1) UPDATE account
   SET  balance = balance - :n
   WHERE account_number = :acc
2) INSERT INTO account_transaction
      (account_number, tran_date, money)
   VALUES ( :acc, :tran_date, :n)
```

In step 1, we update the balance and in step 2, we add a row to the transaction table that appears on our bank statement. Variables prefixed with a colon (:) are program variables of the host program into which the SQL has been embedded.

If step 1 succeeds but, for some reason, step 2 fails, the database will be in an inconsistent state. The balance of the account has been changed, but the corresponding transaction is missing. If step 1 fails but step 2 succeeds, it is equally bad. If neither step is performed, the user might be unhappy but at least the database is intact, and the accounts and transactions are at the same level.

Steps 1 and 2 must be combined into one database transaction, where both steps take place in full or not at all. If either step fails, the other is rolled back. In that case, the ROLLBACK statement is issued, and it appears as if nothing has been done. If both steps are ok, the program will issue a COMMIT statement. This confirms and commits the data into the database. In addition, the rows modified in steps 1 and 2 are locked to prevent other users to read uncommitted data. The locks are only released when the transaction has ended (with either a COMMIT or ROLLBACK).

## 13.2 The ACID Properties of Transactions

A transaction has the following properties:

- **Atomicity**. The entire transaction takes place at once or doesn't happen at all.

- **Consistency**. The database is consistent before and after the transaction (no integrity constraints are violated).

- **Isolation**. The changes made by the transaction are not visible to other transactions until they have been committed, and other transactions, likewise, are not visible to this transaction.

- **Durability**. The changes of a successful transaction remain in the database even in the case of system failure (power failure, disk failure …).

The database management systems maintain a log of all modifications to tables so that they can be backed out in the event of a ROLLBACK or recovered in the event of a system failure.

## 13.3 Transactions in Different Products

All of the products discussed in this book support transaction management. In MySQL, the default table type in the CREATE TABLE statement is MyISAM, which does not have transaction support. You should specify TYPE=InnoDb if you want transaction support in MySQL

In Oracle and DB2, the transaction starts automatically with the first SQL statement. In SQL Server, you must give the BEGIN TRANSACTION statement to begin a transaction. In MySQL and PostgreSQL, you give BEGIN. SQL Server, DB2, Snowflake, and MySQL will, by default, commit after each statement (autocommit).

SQL Server transaction example:

```
BEGIN TRANSACTION
UPDATE account
   SET balance = balance - :n
   WHERE account_number = :acc
INSERT INTO account_transaction (account_number, tran_date,
money)
   VALUES ( :acc, :tran_date, :n)
COMMIT TRANSACTION
```

Similar in Snowflake, but leave out the word "Transaction".

MySQL and PostgreSQL example:

```
BEGIN;
UPDATE account
   SET balance = balance - :n
   WHERE account_number = :acc;
INSERT INTO account_transaction (account_number, tran_date,
money)
   VALUES ( :acc, :tran_date, :n);
COMMIT;
```

A "real" program would have checked the return code after each statement, issued a ROLLBACK, and interrupted the transaction in case of failure.

Oracle and DB2:

```
UPDATE account
   SET balance = balance - :n
   WHERE account_number = :acc;
   COMMIT;
INSERT INTO account_transaction (account_number, tran_date,
money)
   VALUES ( :acc, :tran_date, :n) ;
COMMIT;
```

Let's look at one more example:

```
UPDATE account
   SET balance = balance - :n
   WHERE account_number = :acc;
   COMMIT;
INSERT INTO account_transaction (account_number, tran_date,
money)
   VALUES ( :acc, :tran_date, :n) ;
ROLLBACK;
```

In this example, the account table update was committed, but the account_transaction table was rolled back (just to demonstrate the ROLLBACK statement).

A new transaction always begins after COMMIT and ROLLBACK.

COMMIT and ROLLBACK are used mainly in programs and stored procedures.

Next, an example using the Oracle SQL*Plus interface:

```
SQL> COMMIT;
```

The transaction has been committed.

```
SQL> UPDATE employee
2   SET salary = salary * 1.1
3   WHERE city = 'HELSINKI';
```

2 rows have been updated.

```
SQL> SELECT lname, fname, city, salary FROM employee;

LNAME        FNAME        CITY          SALARY
----------   ----------   ----------    ---------
Stream       Peter        LONDON          2800
Wood         Mike         LONDON          3100
Brooke       Rachel       HELSINKI        3410
Lake         Leon         LONDON          2800
Taylor       Peter        HELSINKI        3256
Brown        Laura        SYDNEY          2650
River        Lilian       SYDNEY          2800
```

7 rows have been chosen.

```
SQL> ROLLBACK;
```

The transaction has been rolled back.

The first COMMIT will finalize the updates to the database up until that point and will release possible locks held by the transaction. This also ends the transaction. The next UPDATE marks the beginning of a new transaction and updates the employee table, but those changes are not yet visible to other users of the database. Other users of the employee table will see it the way it was before the salaries were updated. The salary raise will be visible to others only after the COMMIT of the transaction. If we issue a ROLLBACK statement and undo all changes, then the employee table would be in the same state before our update.

In Oracle, you can give the SET AUTOCOMMIT ON command, after which a COMMIT will be issued for each SQL statement. You can prevent MySQL from automatically committing after each SQL by giving SET AUTOCOMMIT = 0 and in SQL Server with SET IMPLICIT_TRANSACTIONS ON.

Now, these database management products will not commit the data until an explicit COMMIT has been given, so you can group statements into a transaction that is either committed or rolled back in its entirety.

SQL products also do rollbacks on their own. For example, let's assume that the employee table has 100,000 rows, and the update takes some time. Now, there is a problem with the server, perhaps a power failure, and only a part of the rows is updated. When the server is restarted, the database management system will notice that the updated SQL was interrupted (the end of the transaction was not found on the log). The system will return to the original state of the employee table (without the raises) as if no update had ever been done. The integrity of the database remains intact, and we can retry the query.

# CHAPTER FOURTEEN

# Views

Views, or virtual tables, can be thought of as windows into the actual tables. Views do not exist as physical rows. Data is not duplicated in any way. Data is only and always fetched from the underlying tables. Views are treated like actual tables in SQL queries. The description of the view is saved in the system catalog of the database, and when a view is queried, the result is created "on the fly" using the definition of the view and the current values of the underlying tables.

Creating and dropping views requires proper authority.

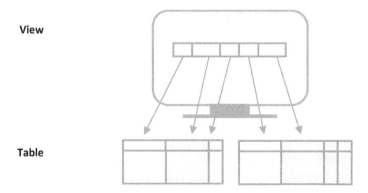

Figure 19: A view is like a window into the data saved in tables. A view as such does not contain any data. All data resides in the tables only.

## 14.1 A View with one Table

*Create the view london for projects located in London.*

```
CREATE VIEW london AS
SELECT projno, project_name, priority, location
FROM project
WHERE location = 'LONDON'
```

Let's try out our new view

```
SELECT *
  FROM london
```

| PROJNO | PROJECT_NAME | PRIORITY | LOCATION |
| ------ | ------------ | -------- | -------- |
| P1 | BOOKKEEPING | 2 | LONDON |
| P4 | ACCOUNTING | 2 | LONDON |

The system fetched these rows from the project table through the london view. If somebody went and changed the rows in the project table, the user of the london view would always get fresh up-to-date data on the projects. You can think of views as "canned queries" which are activated each time the view is used.

Practically any **SELECT, UPDATE, INSERT,** and **DELETE** statement can target the london view, for example:

```
SELECT project_name
FROM london
WHERE project_name like 'B%'
ORDER BY project_name
```

| PROJECT_NAME |
| ------------ |
| BOOKKEEPING |

When building views, first make the select statement. When you are satisfied with the result, add "CREATE VIEW …" to the top.

Views often use only a subset of the columns. The columns can be given new names by listing them in parentheses after the name of the view.

Let's create the view emp_public, which contains all information about the employees except for the salary and the tax rate, which we want to keep secret. We will also rename some columns to make them more descriptive and reorder them.

```
CREATE VIEW emp_public
(lastname, firstname, empno, education,
        start_date, city,  deptno) AS
SELECT  lname, fname, empno, education,
        start_date, city, deptno
FROM employee
```

Let's test our new view.

```
SELECT *
FROM emp_public
```

| lastname | firstname | empno | education | start_date | city | deptno |
|----------|-----------|-------|-----------|------------|------|--------|
| Stream | Peter | 2134 | Ba | 2020-03-02 00:00:00.000 | LONDON | 3 |
| Wood | Mike | 2234 | PhD | 2009-10-15 00:00:00.000 | LONDON | 1 |
| Brooke | Rachel | 2245 | MA | 2014-09-24 00:00:00.000 | HELSINKI | 4 |
| Lake | Leon | 2345 | NULL | 2018-01-01 00:00:00.000 | LONDON | 3 |
| Taylor | Peter | 2884 | MA | 2009-05-12 00:00:00.000 | HELSINKI | NULL |
| Brown | Laura | 3546 | Ba | 2017-09-15 00:00:00.000 | SYDNEY | 1 |
| River | Lilian | 3547 | DIP | 2009-05-12 00:00:00.000 | SYDNEY | 3 |

Now, we can give public permissions to this view so that everybody can see employees, without salaries and tax rates. The users actually do not have to know whether it is a view or a table.

**EXERCISES**

1.  Create the view v_hels for employees from Helsinki. Add the following columns in this order: lname, fname, empno, city, and start_date. Try out your new view.

---

## 14.2 Complex Views

A view can be a window into several tables at the same time. For instance, the join of two or more tables. Views are often used to hide the complexity of an underlying SQL statement. A complex query is made easy for the end user to use.

*Create a view that gives us directly all project information, including the total and estimated hours worked and their difference per project.*

```
CREATE VIEW project_status (projno, project_name, priority,
   hours_act_tot, hours_diff)
AS
SELECT p.projno, p.project_name, p.priority,
   SUM(pe.hours_act), SUM(pe.hours_est) - SUM(pe.hours_act)
FROM project p
LEFT JOIN proj_emp pe
  ON p.projno = pe.projno
GROUP BY p.projno, p.project_name, p.priority
```

Now, even the project manager (who has not yet taken the SQL advanced course) can query the project status:

```
SELECT *
FROM project_status
ORDER BY projno
```

| PROJNO | PROJECTNAME | PRIORITY | HOURS_ACT_TOT | HOURS_DIFF |
|--------|-------------|----------|---------------|------------|
| P1 | BOOKKEEPING | 2 | 1600 | 0 |
| P2 | BILLING | 1 | 700 | -200 |
| P3 | WAREHOUSING | 3 | 900 | -800 |
| P4 | ACCOUNTING | 2 | 900 | 300 |
| P5 | CUSTOMERS | 3 | NULL | NULL |
| P6 | STATISTICS | NULL | NULL | NULL |

As in the above example, views often consist of multi-table join queries. A database that is well designed, where tables are in the so-called third normal form, will contain many tables with a few columns each. With views, we can recombine tables into bigger entities. The normalization will be "hidden" from the user. In fact, we are denormalizing.

Sometimes, such wide, easy-to-use tables are called One Big Table (OBT), which here we implement as a view instead of a physical table. The performance of the view should be the same as the query in the view definition.

**EXERCISES**

1. Create the view v_proj_hours with a row for each project and the following columns: projno, project_name, and hours_total. Tip: first make the query and when it works, add the CREATE VIEW statement on top.

2. Create view v_projects which gives information on projects and project employees: project number, project name, employee number and name, and actual hours per project (not summed). Use a SELECT from the view to list projects: project_name, lname, fname, hours_act. Order by project_name, lname. Then use the view to list all employees and their projects: lname, fname, project_name, hours_act. Sort to make it readable.

## 14.3 SQL View Rules

A view can be based on another view or view, so it is permissible to pile views on top of each other. You can join a table with a view and a view with a view. Use any SQL query you like to define a view, but you mustn't include the ORDER BY clause in the query. To order the output, use ORDER BY in the final query that uses the view.

 It is useful to add unions of several tables in a view (SELECT UNION SELECT UNION etc.). This way it looks like the data of several tables are all in one table.

Changing a view is easy: DROP the existing view and recreate it with the changed definition. Dropping a view does not delete any rows. However, the possible permissions given to use the view will be lost.

## 14.4 Updating Tables via a View

In general, it is best to update table data directly and not through views. Anyway, there are restrictions on how you can update data (insert, delete, update) via a view. Generally speaking, an update is only possible for views that refer to only one table, and even then, the following conditions apply:

- DISTINCT not used
- No functions or calculations in the columns of the SELECT list (e.g., salary/30)
- WHERE clause does not contain a subquery
- no GROUP BY clause
- no HAVING clause
- FROM clause contains only one table – no updating of views that contain joins

These restrictions are based on the ANSI standard. Many SQL products have more degrees of freedom. For example, in SQL Server, you can update a table with values from another table using a view with join.

You can rename existing columns in a view, as we did in the previous example. You have to give a name to those columns that result from invoking functions or are a result of calculations (e.g., salary*12.5). If two columns have the same name (this can happen in joins), one must be renamed. For instance, the following view definition will give an error because SUM(hours_act) cannot be the name of a column.

```
CREATE VIEW hours_actual                 -- Error!
AS
    SELECT projno, SUM(hours_act)
    FROM proj_emp
    GROUP BY projno
```

Give each column a new name in parentheses after the view name.

```
CREATE VIEW hours_actual (projno, actual_hours)
AS
    SELECT projno, SUM(hours_act)
    FROM proj_emp
    GROUP BY projno
```

Or, alternatively, you can give an alias name to the column:

```
CREATE VIEW hours_actual
AS
    SELECT projno, SUM(hours_act) AS actual_hours
    FROM proj_emp
    GROUP BY projno
```

## 14.5 Check Option

A rarely used option, the WITH CHECK OPTION, will prevent updates through the view that don't conform to the conditions in the WHERE clause. You can use this option to prevent invalid values from entering the table.

*Create a view that restricts the value of the priority column in the project table to 1, 2,3, or 4.*

```
CREATE VIEW v_proj
   AS
SELECT * FROM project
WHERE priority IN (1,2,3,4)
WITH CHECK OPTION
```

Now, it is impossible to update the priority to something else as values 1, 2, 3, or 4 when using the view v_proj.

A CHECK option defined directly in the table is a better way to enforce legal values than the WITH CHECK OPTION in views, since it can't be bypassed.

## 14.6 Dropping Views

You can drop a view at any time using the DROP VIEW statement.

*Drop view emp_public.*

```
DROP VIEW emp_public
```

Dropping a view does not in any way affect the underlying tables or the data in these tables. Other views that were defined in this view will either disappear or be marked as invalid but not removed. Permissions given to the view will be lost.

## 14.7 Synonyms and Aliases

You can give additional names to a table using synonyms or aliases. Synonyms and/or aliases are available in most products.

The owner of the table can reference the table by just using the name of the table. If you want to reference a table owned by somebody else, you must prefix the name with the name of the owner (and, of course, have the appropriate privileges). The same goes for views.

In this example, a user other than "edu" is referencing a table owned by "edu":

```
SELECT *
FROM edu.project

projno project_name        priority location
------ ---------------     -------- ----------
P1     BOOKKEEPING              2    LONDON
P2     BILLING                  1    HELSINKI
P3     WAREHOUSING              3    HELSINKI
P4     ACCOUNTING               2    LONDON
P5     CUSTOMERS                3    SINGAPORE
P6     STATISTICS            NULL    NULL
```

To minimize the amount of typing, we can create a synonym for that table (not in Hive, PostgreSQL, and MySQL):

```
CREATE SYNONYM pro
FOR edu.project
```

Now we can simply reference the synonym:

```
SELECT *
FROM pro
```

A synonym is removed using the DROP statement:

```
DROP SYNONYM pro
```

In Hive, PostgreSQL, and MySQL, you can use views to get similar results.

# CHAPTER 15

# Indexes

This chapter will show you how to create and remove indexes. Indexes enhance the efficiency of queries.

## 15.1 What is an index?

One of the basic principles of SQL is that you can search for data using any set of columns. In this sense, all columns are "created equal". However, performance may vary significantly depending on which columns are used in the WHERE clause. Query performance is often enhanced by creating indexes for columns.

An index in SQL functions like an index in a book. It is ordered and contains pointers to the corresponding rows in the table. The structure is usually a B-tree or hash-based. This allows the needed rows to be located quickly using the index, and the actual data is also accessed swiftly from the table via direct pointers.

For more details on indexes and the optimizer, refer to Chapter 22.

An index can be created directly after the creation of the table, or when the table contains rows, provided you have the correct privileges.

An index can be dropped at any time without altering the SQL statements embedded in programs or given interactively in any way. Indexes only affect performance.

Indexes are not referenced in SQL statements. Thus, by examining a statement, we cannot determine if it uses a specific index or not. This allows performance enhancement by creating or removing indexes without modifying programs. This is great, as you can tune your database for better performance without altering any programs or code!

You can view the indexes created for each table by examining the system catalog (see Chapter 17).

Indexes have the following functions:

- Unique indexes enforce the uniqueness of rows
    - typically Primary keys, but other columns can be unique as well
- Speeding up queries
    - indexes for condition columns in the WHERE clause
    - usually, indexes are created for foreign keys to speed joins
    - often an index contains several columns
    - so-called covering indexes contain all the columns that are referenced in the query; the help to obtain very good performance.
- Avoid sorting
    - an index is already in order so an explicit sort can be avoided

Snowflake and Hive do not use indexes due to their special internal structure.

Index design requires expertise. Before creating one, you should consult a database administrator.

Indexes might also be harmful. They take up space. Because they are automatically maintained, a table with too many indexes might be slow to update. Only create indexes that you find useful to speed up queries.

## 15.2 Creating an Index

If your application has a name search (which is typical), it is a good idea to create an index to support it.

```
CREATE INDEX employee_name ON employee(lname, fname)
```

This index speeds up queries like:

```
SELECT * FROM employee
WHERE lname = 'Smith'
```

Or:

```
SELECT * FROM employee
WHERE lname = 'Smith' AND fname = 'Adam'
```

Look for more information in Chapter 22.3.

SQL databases create automatically unique indexes for primary keys. An exception is DB2, where you must create them yourself, this way:

```
CREATE UNIQUE INDEX employee_pk ON employee(empno)
CREATE UNIQUE INDEX proj_emp_pk ON proj_emp(empno,projno)
```

The UNIQUE specification ensures that no duplicates are entered into tables. For instance, you cannot save two employees with the same empno. You can define it for any column that needs to be unique.

---

### 15.3 Removing an Index

An index can be removed at any time (without having to modify programs or SQL statements).

Let's assume that we don't need to search for employees by name very often after all, so to speed up updates we drop the index.

```
DROP INDEX employee_name
```

The only time we use the name of the index is when we are creating or dropping one. SQL statements never refer to the name of the index. The optimizer of the system decides which indexes to use to obtain the fastest access plan. The task of the index designer is to create suitable indexes so that the optimizer can end up using them.

# CHAPTER SIXTEEN

# Privileges

Querying data with SQL is quite easy (at least after reading this book :), so it is important to protect the data from the unauthorized. The database and security administrators usually take care of privileges, here we just quickly go over the main principles.

SQL contains the tools to allow or inhibit the reading or updating data by user and table. Different users can be given different privileges to the same table. For instance, user A might be allowed to only read a table, while user B can both read and update that same table. Privileges are also needed to create and remove tables. Typically, database administrators (DBA) have the widest privileges.

The creator of a table always has all privileges for it. Others have to be granted privileges separately.

Granting privileges is based on three factors:

- **Users**. Always when connecting to a database, you have to give your user ID and password. Privileges are given to users.

- **Database objects**. These are tables, columns, views and all other objects that you can create in a database. Privileges are granted on objects.

- **Privileges**. Privileges specify what operations a user can do to a specific database object. The operations for tables include SELECT, UPDATE, DELETE, and INSERT.

---

## 16.1 Users and Roles

When a database management system is installed, it usually has a set of default users. Let's use Oracle as an example. Oracle has the users SYS and SYSTEM. SYS is the most powerful user. It owns, for instance, the system catalog tables. SYSTEM is the user with database administrator (DBA) privileges. SYSTEM can be used to create new user ids for people who need to manage the database. In SQL Server, the default superuser is "sa". When the DBA has created a new user, it has to grant this user privileges to objects that the user needs to access.

A role is a set of privileges that have been bundled together. If you grant a role to a user, the user automatically obtains all privileges included in the role. For example, the sysadmin role in SQL Server grants you access to all objects and functions. The purpose of roles is to ease the work of DBAs.

In Oracle, a user is created and the password is altered as follows (the user is "edu" with DBA authorities):

```
CREATE USER Peter  IDENTIFIED BY pw1
ALTER USER Peter   IDENTIFIED BY pw2
```

Peter needs these privileges to connect to the database:

```
GRANT CONNECT, RESOURCE TO Peter;
```

Peter still can't access the tables:

```
SELECT fname, lname
FROM edu.employee

ORA-00942: table or view does not exist
```

We must grant him privileges to the table:

```
GRANT SELECT, INSERT ON employee TO Peter;
```

Now, Peter can query the employee table and add rows to it.

Then we revoke the privileges from Peter and remove Peter as a user:

```
REVOKE SELECT, INSERT ON employee FROM Peter;
DROP USER Peter;
```

In SQL Server, a user is created, and the password is modified like this:

```
EXEC sp_addlogin 'Peter', 'pw1'
EXEC sp_password 'pw1', 'pw2' , 'Peter'
```

We grant Peter access to the database:

```
EXEC sp_grantdbaccess 'Peter'
```

After this, we can grant privileges to Peter.

## 16.2 Examples

We will show some more examples of using GRANT and REVOKE, which belong to ANSI standard.

In the chapter on views, we created the view emp_public based on the table employee to hide sensitive salary data. Now, we complete the task.

*Grant only users Tom and Mary the privileges to the employee table. Hence, they are the only ones allowed to see the salaries.*

```
GRANT SELECT ON employees TO Tom, Mary
```

*In addition, Mary can maintain (add and update) data in employee (but not remove rows).*

```
GRANT INSERT, UPDATE ON employee TO Mary
```

*Allow all users to view the data in the view emp_public, the view of the employee table with the salary data removed. In this way, everybody can access personnel data (except for the salary).*

```
GRANT SELECT ON emp_public TO PUBLIC
```

*Grant the user Jack all privileges on the employee table. This consists of the SELECT, INSERT, DELETE, and UPDATE privileges. In addition, give Jack the privilege to further grant these privileges (given with the WITH GRANT OPTION clause).*

```
GRANT ALL ON employee TO Jack
WITH GRANT OPTION
```

"GRANT ALL" can also be stated as:

```
GRANT ALL PRIVILEGES
```

Only Mary can update the priorities of projects.

```
GRANT UPDATE (priority) ON project TO Mary
```

Tom and Mary get reassigned to new tasks and their privileges are revoked:

```
REVOKE ALL ON employee FROM Tom, Mary
```

Note that the revoking of privileges from a user will cascade to the users that have been further granted privileges by that user (WITH GRANT OPTION in reverse).

# CHAPTER SEVENTEEN

# System Catalog

The database management system must keep track of all tables, columns, indexes, and other database objects it includes. This so-called metadata is saved in the system catalog (data dictionary). The system catalog consists of a set of tables, so data about data is also saved in tables. Being a SQL system, it can be queried with SQL just as any "normal" table.

The ANSI standard defines quite specifically what columns and data each system catalog table should contain. This is called the Information Schema. Unfortunately, not all the products adhere to this standard, and the naming and structure of the system catalog differ for many products. We will introduce the main features of the system catalogs product by product. For each product, there exist handy graphical interfaces that can be used to browse the databases, tables, columns, and other metadata.

## 17.1 Oracle's System Catalog Tables

The Oracle System Catalog contains many different tables and views. We look at some of the most important ones. The Oracle System Catalog Tables are described in the view DICT.

Oracle's System Catalog Tables are always prefixed by one of the following:

```
USER      shows the current user's objects only
ALL       all objects that are accessible by the user
DBA       the DBA view (all objects)
```

For instance, let's select all tables owned by the current user:

```
SELECT table_name
FROM user_tables;
```

Here are some other useful tables (remember the prefixes ALL_ and DBA_):

```
USER_INDEXES          Indexes
USER_SEQUENCES        Sequences
USER_TABLES           Tables
USER_TAB_COLUMNS      Columns
USER_CATALOG          Tables, views, synonyms and sequences
USER_USERS            Users
USER_VIEWS            Views
```

The columns for one table or view can be listed easily with the SQL*Plus command DESC:

```
SQL> DESC employee
Name                                               NULLS?    Type
-------------------------------------------------- -------- ------------
EMPNO                                              NOT NULL CHAR(4)
FNAME                                                       VARCHAR2(40)
LNAME                                                       VARCHAR2(40)
CITY                                                        VARCHAR2(40)
EDUCATION                                                   CHAR(8)
SALARY                                                      NUMBER(7,2)
TAX_RATE                                                    NUMBER(3,1)
START_DATE                                                  DATE
DEPTNO                                                      NUMBER(6)
```

You can get all tables and views in a database from the handy 'tab' view:

```
SELECT *
FROM tab

TNAME                               TABTYPE  CLUSTERID
----------------------------------- -------- ----------
DEPARTMENT                          TABLE
EMPLOYEE                            TABLE
EMP_PUBLIC                          VIEW
...
```

All tables that contain a column of a certain name:

```
SELECT TABLE_NAME
FROM USER_TAB_COLUMNS
WHERE COLUMN_NAME = 'PROJNO'

TABLE_NAME
--------------
PROJECT
PROJEMP
PROJ_HIST
...
```

In the graphical SQL Developer tool, you can see tables, columns, etc., in a object browser.

---

## 17.2 System Catalog of SQL Server, Snowflake and PostgreSQL

Use the views of the INFORMATION_SCHEMA as defined by the ANSI standard. The most important views are:

```
INFORMATION_SCHEMA.TABLES            Tables
INFORMATION_SCHEMA.COLUMNS           Columns
INFORMATION_SCHEMA.KEY_COLUMN_USAGE  Foreign and primary keys
INFORMATION_SCHEMA.VIEWS             Views
```

For instance, the following query shows the structure of the employee table:

```
SELECT table_name,  column_name, column_default,
       data_type, character_maximum_length AS max_length
FROM information_schema.columns
WHERE table_name = 'EMPLOYEE'
```

| table_name | column_name | column_default | data_type | max_length |
| --- | --- | --- | --- | --- |
| employee | empno | NULL | char | 4 |
| employee | fname | NULL | varchar | 40 |
| employee | lname | NULL | varchar | 40 |
| employee | city | NULL | varchar | 40 |
| employee | education | NULL | char | 8 |
| employee | salary | NULL | decimal | NULL |
| employee | tax_rate | NULL | decimal | NULL |
| employee | start_date | NULL | datetime | NULL |
| employee | deptno | NULL | smallint | NULL |

In PostgreSQL, you can list the tables with the following query:

```
SELECT *
FROM pg_catalog.pg_tables
```

SQL Server has a set of useful system procedures for viewing the System Catalogue. Here are some of them:

```
sp_tables                    database tables and views
sp_columns 'employee'        columns for the employee table
sp_help                      all objects in the database
sp_help 'employee'           information from table 'employee'
sp_helpindex 'employee'      information from 'employee' indexes
sp_who                       users currently logged on to the
                             database
```

In SQL Server, you can use the graphical SQL Management Studio, which is a schema browser for tables, columns, etc. In PostgreSQL, you can use pgAdmin. In Snowflake, use Snowsight.

## 17.3 DB2 System Catalog

Here are some of the tables of the DB2 System Catalog:

```
SYSCAT.TABLES          Tables
SYSCAT.COLUMNS         Columns
SYSCAT.VIEWS           Views
SYSCAT.TABAUTH         Table level privileges
SYSCAT.INDEXES         Indexes
SYSCAT.INDEXCOLUSE     Index columns
```

Let's find out which tables contain a column called PROJNO:

```
SELECT tabname, colname
FROM syscat.columns
WHERE colname = 'PROJNO'


TABNAME          COLNAME
-----------      -------
PROJECT          PROJNO
PROJ_EMP         PROJNO

...
```

Columns of the employee table:

```
SELECT tabname, colname, typename, length, scale, nulls
FROM syscat.columns
WHERE tabname = 'EMPLOYEE'
ORDER BY colno
```

| TABNAME | COLNAME | TYPENAME | LENGTH | SCALE | NULLS |
|---------|---------|----------|--------|-------|-------|
| EMPLOYEE | EMPNO | CHARACTER | 4 | 0 | N |
| EMPLOYEE | FNAME | VARCHAR | 40 | 0 | Y |
| EMPLOYEE | LNAME | VARCHAR | 40 | 0 | Y |
| EMPLOYEE | CITY | VARCHAR | 40 | 0 | Y |
| EMPLOYEE | EDUCATION | CHARACTER | 8 | 0 | Y |
| EMPLOYEE | SALARY | DECIMAL | 7 | 2 | Y |
| EMPLOYEE | TAX_RATE | DECIMAL | 3 | 1 | Y |
| EMPLOYEE | START_DATE | DATE | 4 | 0 | Y |
| EMPLOYEE | DEPTNO | SMALLINT | 2 | 0 | Y |

The DESCRIBE command can also be used, for instance:

```
DESCRIBE TABLE project
```

| Column | Skema | Datatype | Len | Dec | NULLS |
|--------|-------|----------|-----|-----|-------|
| PROJNO | SYSIBM | VARCHAR | 4 | 0 | No |
| PROJECT_NAME | SYSIBM | VARCHAR | 50 | 0 | Yes |
| PRIORITY | SYSIBM | SMALLINT | 2 | 0 | Yes |
| LOCATION | SYSIBM | VARCHAR | 15 | 0 | Yes |

## 17.4 MySQL System Catalog

The MySQL System Catalog can be queried as follows:

```
SHOW TABLES            database tables
SHOW COLUMNS FROM      columns for a table (see example below)
SHOW INDEX             indexes for a table (see example below)
SHOW STATUS            information on the state of the server
SHOW TABLE STATUS      technical data (e.g. number of rows)
DESCRIBE or DESC       as SHOW COLUMNS
SHOW CREATE TABLE      shows the CREATE TABLE statement for the
                       table


SHOW COLUMNS FROM employee

Field  Type         Null  Key  Default  Extra
-----  -----------  ----  ---  -------  -----
empno  varchar(4)         PRI
fname  varchar(40)  YES        NULL
lname  varchar(40)  YES        NULL
city   varchar(40)  YES        NULL
. . .
```

**DESC** employee will give the same result.

The following command will show the indexes for the employee table:

```
SHOW INDEX FROM employee
```

Show the CREATE TABLE statement for a given table.

```
SHOW CREATE TABLE employee
CREATE TABLE `employee` (
  `empno` varchar(4) NOT NULL default '',
  `fname` varchar(40) default NULL,
  `lname` varchar(40) default NULL,
  `city` varchar(40) default NULL,
  `education` varchar(8) default NULL,
  `salary` decimal(7,2) default NULL,
  `tax_rate` decimal(3,1) default NULL,
  `start_date` datetime default NULL,
  `deptno` smallint(6) default NULL,
  PRIMARY KEY  (`empno`),
  KEY `deptno` (`deptno`),
  CONSTRAINT `0_34` FOREIGN KEY (`deptno`) REFERENCES
`department` (`deptno`) ON DELETE SET NULL
) TYPE=InnoDB DEFAULT CHARSET=latin1
```

The MySQL Workbench and phpMyAdmin tools can be used to browse the catalog and also run queries.

# CHAPTER EIGHTEEN

# Advanced Functions and Strings

This chapter shows examples of more complex functions and string manipulations.

## 18.1 NULL Handling, Conditional Reasoning and Converting

We will introduce three handy functions that are part of the ANSI standard and, hence, work in all the products of this book. They are COALESCE, CASE, and CAST.

### COALESCE NULL-Function

NULL was introduced in an earlier chapter. Now, we will dive deeper. Calculations with NULL values always produce a NULL value. So, a common requirement is to convert a NULL to zero.

*Calculate the difference between the actual hours and planned hours for project P1.*

```
SELECT  projno, empno, hours_est, hours_act,
        hours_est - hours_act AS diff
FROM proj_emp
WHERE projno = 'P1'
ORDER BY projno, empno


PROJNO EMPNO HOURS_EST HOURS_ACT   DIFF
------ ----- --------- ----------  ----
P1     2134        300        300     0
P1     2234       NULL        200  NULL  ←
P1     2245        300        200   100
P1     2345        100        100     0
P1     2884        200        100   100
P1     3546        500        400   100
P1     3547        200        300  -100
```

The difference for employee 2234 is NULL because NULL minus 200 is NULL. However, we are assuming that in the case of NULL, the number of planned hours is 0. With the COALESCE function, we can convert NULL to zero (if the value is not NULL, the value will remain the same).

```
SELECT  projno, empno, hours_est, hours_act,
        COALESCE(hours_est, 0)- hours_act AS diff
FROM proj_emp
WHERE projno = 'P1'
ORDER BY projno, empno


PROJNO EMPNO HOURS_EST HOURS_ACT   DIFF
------ ----- --------- ----------  ----
P1     2134        300        300     0
P1     2234       NULL        200  -200   ←
P1     2245        300        200   100
P1     2345        100        100     0
P1     2884        200        100   100
P1     3546        500        400   100
P1     3547        200        300  -100
```

COALESCE adheres to the ANSI standard. There are some similar product-specific functions available, some of which are shown in the table below. You might find them in existing SQL statements, and of course, you can still use them.

| VALUE (hours_est, 0) | DB2 |
| --- | --- |
| NVL (hours_est, 0) | Oracle, Snowflake, Hive |
| ISNULL (hours_est, 0) | SQL Server, MySQL |

Another example of the usage of COALESCE:

*Get projno, project_name, and location from the project table. If location is missing (is NULL), mark it with the text <not found>.*

```
SELECT projno, project_name,
        COALESCE (location, '<not found>') AS location
FROM project

PROJNO    PROJECT_NAME    LOCATION
------    ------------    --------
P1        BOOKKEEPING     LONDON
P2        BILLING         HELSINKI
P3        WAREHOUSING     PARIS
P4        ACCOUNTING      LONDON
P5        CUSTOMERS       SINGAPORE
P6        STATISTICS      <not found>
```

## EXERCISES

1.  Get project name, priority, and location for all projects. If the priority is NULL, replace it with a zero. If the location is NULL, replace it with the text 'no location'.

## Conditional Reasoning with CASE

CASE is a handy construct that was introduced in the SQL-92 standard and is available in practically all SQL products. It is like the IF THEN ELSE construct available in programming languages. CASE can be used for conditional reasoning. In the following example, we define two columns with the help of the CASE construct. The column expression starts with the keyword CASE and ends with END after which we can specify a column alias as usual. The query below has four columns, two of which include conditions expressed with CASE.

*Fetch all projects with the number, name, and country based on city and priority in clear text.*

```
SELECT  projno,
        project_name,
        CASE location              -- CASE syntax type 1
           WHEN 'HELSINKI' THEN 'FINLAND'
           WHEN 'LONDON' THEN 'ENGLAND'
           ELSE 'OTHER'
        END AS country,
        CASE                       -- CASE syntax type 2
           WHEN priority <= 2 THEN 'IMPORTANT'
           WHEN priority = 3 THEN 'NOT SO IMPORTANT'
           ELSE 'UNKNOWN IMPORTANCE'
        END AS prio_class
FROM project
ORDER BY projno

PROJNO PROJECT_NAME       COUNTRY PRIO_CLASS
------ ----------------   ------- ------------------
P1     BOOKKEEPING        ENGLAND IMPORTANT
P2     BILLING            FINLAND IMPORTANT
P3     WAREHOUSING        FINLAND NOT SO IMPORTANT
P4     ACCOUNTING         ENGLAND IMPORTANT
P5     CUSTOMERS          OTHER   NOT SO IMPORTANT
P6     STATISTICS         OTHER   UNKNOWN IMPORTANCE
```

CASE has two distinct syntaxes, see the example above. In the first form, we compare the equality of values to the expression after the CASE keyword (type 1. CASE syntax). In the other case, the whole conditional expression is given after each WHEN keyword, as with the column prio_class (type 2. CASE syntax). We use the latter form in cases where equality is not involved or when we are comparing it with NULL. For instance, the following example will not work if we convert NULL to the text "not found":

```
SELECT projno,            -- will not convert NULLs properly
       project_name,
       CASE location
          WHEN NULL THEN 'not found'
          ELSE location
       END AS location
FROM project
```

This form of CASE (type 1) works only when testing equality, and since "location = NULL" is never true, it will not give the correct result. We must use the format that gives the whole condition, that is type 2:

```
SELECT projno,
       project_name,
       CASE
          WHEN location IS NULL THEN 'not found'
          ELSE location
       END AS location
FROM project

PROJNO PROJECT_NAME LOCATION
------ ------------ ----------------
P1     BOOKKEEPING  LONDON
P2     BILLING      HELSINKI
P3     WAREHOUSING  HELSINKI
P4     ACCOUNTING   LONDON
P5     CUSTOMERS    SINGAPORE
P6     STATISTICS   not found
```

CASE can also be used in the WHERE and UPDATE clauses.

COALESCE can be replaced with CASE (although not recommended, COALESCE is easier):

```
SELECT  projno, empno, hours_est, hours_act,
        CASE
            WHEN hours_est IS NULL THEN 0
            ELSE hours_est
        END hours_act AS diff
FROM proj_emp
WHERE projno = 'P1'
```

**EXERCISES**

1. Get project name, priority, and, depending on the priority, the following text:

   'top' if the priority is 1

   'important' if the priority is 2

   'normal' if the priority is 3

   'don't care' for others

   Order by project name.

2. We are creating input to another system. For that reason, we need to put the salaries in two different columns: for LOWSAL salaries 2800 or less and HIGHSAL salaries over 2800, see below. The salary is zero if it appears in the other column. Order by last name.

```
lname      lowsal        highsal
--------   ----------    --------
Brooke     0.00          3100.00
Brown      2650.00       0.00
Lake       2800.00       0.00
River      2800.00       0.00
Stream     2800.00       0.00
Taylor     0.00          2960.00
Wood       0.00          3100.00
```

## CAST for Data Type Conversions

Data type conversions of an expression are often needed, such as a conversion from numeric to character. Dates and timestamps are also often converted to character strings, and character strings containing a numeric value can be converted to numeric. CAST is a handy conversion function that originated from the SQL-92 standard and works in all our SQL products. Here are some examples:

```
CAST(start_date AS CHAR(20))       -- convert date to character
CAST(empno AS DECIMAL)             -- character string to numeric
CAST(salary/30 AS DECIMAL (7,2)) -- daily salary to decimal
CAST(deptno AS CHAR(5))            -- numeric deptno to character
```

*Fetch last name, empno, empno as numeric, and salary as a character string for those employees whose salary starts with the number (or character) '3'.*

```
SELECT lname,
       empno,
       CAST(empno AS DECIMAL) AS numeric_empno,
       CAST(salary AS CHAR(10)) AS character_salary
FROM employee
WHERE SUBSTRING(CAST(salary AS CHAR(10)), 1, 1) = '3'
          -- in Oracle, DB2 use SUBSTR
```

```
LNAME       EMPNO NUMERIC_EMPNO     CHARACTER_SALARY
-----       ----- -------------     ----------------
Wood        2234  2234              3100
Brooke      2245  2245              3100
```

SUBSTRING and SUBSTR functions can only be used for character strings, so we first converted the salary to a string.

There are also product-specific functions for data type conversions. See some examples in the table below. For more information, consult your product documentation.

| | |
|---|---|
| `TO_CHAR(priority)`<br>`TO_NUMBER(empno)`<br>`TO_DATE('15.09.2024', 'DD.MM.YYYY')` | Oracle, Snowflake, PostgreSQL |
| `CONVERT(CHAR(5), priority),`<br>`STR(priority)` | SQL Server |
| `CHAR(priority), DIGITS(priority)` | DB2 |

## EXERCISES

1. Write a SELECT query that adds one (+1) to the empno of all employees. The datatype of empno is CHAR(4), so you must first convert the value to an integer. In the same query, change the start_date to the data type character CHAR(20). Include the original values in the query as separate columns. Order by lname.

## 18.2 Special Cases of Character Searches

If you are searching for a character string with a single quotation mark (') you have to use two sequential quotation marks in the search string.

*Get departments with the code s'sdfg\*234.*

```
SELECT * FROM department
WHERE code = 's''dfg*234'

DEPTNO DEPTNAME    CODE
------ ---------   -------------
     2 Economy     s'dfg*234
```

Use the same method to add a value into a column with INSERT (two quotation marks).

A quotation mark in a result might cause problems since it might be seen to denote the end of a string. In the following example, the REPLACE function is used to replace the quotation marks with a '+'.

SQL Server:

```
SELECT deptno, deptname, code,
          REPLACE (code, 0x27, '+') AS quote_replaced
FROM department
WHERE  deptno = 2

DEPTNO  CODE         QUOTE_REPLACED
------- -----------  ---------------
     2  s'dfg*234    s+dfg*234
```

If you want to use LIKE to search for the special characters % or _, use the ESCAPE clause to specify an escape character. After the escape character, you can give either % or _.

*Fetch departments whose code contains the string 'a_'.*

```
SELECT *
FROM department
WHERE CODE LIKE '%a#_%'  ESCAPE '#'

DEPTNO DEPTNAME   CODE
------ ---------- -----------
1      IT         asa_123456
3      Research   a_ss*8888
```

The hash character # is used to express that character underscore _ is being searched for, which would otherwise be reserved for a single character search.

---

## 18.3 Find the First Word of a String

Sometimes, we need to extract strings in a dynamic fashion. We can build the SUBSTRING function to do this.

The following example shows how to find the first word of the department name. We first search for the position of the first blank and then use SUBSTR or SUBSTRING to extract the first word by setting the parameters as follows: start is position 1 and length is the location of the first blank. The separate first blank location column (see below) is unnecessary but is shown here for clarity. The important column is the 3rd column, first_word.

Let's assume that the name of department 1 is 'IT Development'.

DB2:

```
SELECT deptname,
   LOCATE(' ',deptname ) AS pos,    -- location of first blank
   SUBSTR(deptname,1 , LOCATE(' ',deptname )) AS first_word
FROM department
WHERE deptname LIKE '% %'     -- only rows with a blank or more


DEPTNAME        POS        FIRST_WORD
--------------- ---------- ----------
IT Development  3          IT
```

Oracle:

```
SELECT deptname,
   INSTR(deptname, ' ' ) AS pos,     -- location of first blank
   SUBSTR(deptname,1 ,  INSTR(deptname, ' ' )) AS first_word
FROM department
WHERE deptname LIKE '% %'     -- only rows with a blank or more
```

SQL Server and Snowflake:

```
SELECT deptname,
  CHARINDEX(' ', deptname) AS pos, -- location of first blank
   SUBSTRING(deptname,1,CHARINDEX(' ',deptname)-1) AS first_word
FROM department
WHERE deptname LIKE '% %'      -- only rows with a blank or more
```

PostgreSQL, MySQL:

```
SELECT deptname,
   POSITION(' ' IN deptname) AS pos,   -- location of first blank
   SUBSTR(deptname,1 , POSITION(' ' IN deptname)) AS first_word
FROM department
WHERE deptname LIKE '% %'       -- only rows with a blank or more
```

---

### 18.4 Adding Leading Zeros

Sometimes, we must add leading zeros to numbers where they have disappeared. For instance, zip codes that are numeric. If data comes from an Excel spreadsheet, leading zeros are often lost. The zip code 00501 might become 501 and 33511 will come out correctly. We need to add the leading zeroes so that the final length of the value is always five. We try to simulate the situation with the last names:

*Generate strings of length six from the last names so that the missing characters are added as leading zeroes (for instance, Wood becomes 00Wood). This is the result:*

```
str
------
Stream
00Wood
Brooke
00Lake
Taylor
0Brown
0River
```

Below, we have used two methods. The first one adds a maximum number of leading zeros (6) to the name and then takes the six rightmost characters from the result so that the extra zeroes will get cut off. Some products have an LPAD function, which will pad the start of the string with a character of your choice.

DB2 and Snowflake:

```
SELECT RIGHT('000000' || lname, 6 ) AS str
FROM employee
```

SQL Server:

```
SELECT RIGHT('000000' + lname, 6 ) AS str
FROM employee
```

Oracle, PostgreSQL, Snowflake, MySQL, Hive:

```
SELECT LPAD(lname, 6, '0') AS str
FROM employee                    -- pads with zeroes from left
```

Or in Oracle:

```
SELECT SUBSTR('000000' ||lname, -6,6) AS str
FROM employee;
```

---

### 18.5 How to Extract Year + Month from a Date

Sometimes, we need a date converted to a string with the year and month concatenated, especially in summary tables. For instance, the date 2023-01-01 would become 202301 and the date 2019-12-16 would become 201912. This is a good format, easy to sort, easy to filter to one year, and works for pivoting headers.

A typical use is in data warehousing, where you maintain a monthly aggregate table of transactions. Below is also the INSERT SELECT format.

*Fetch salaries summarized by employment year and month, with the columns yyyymm and tot_salary.*

Oracle, Snowflake, DB2 LUW, PostgreSQL:

```
SELECT TO_CHAR(start_date, 'YYYYMM')  AS year_mon,
              SUM(salary) AS tot_salary
FROM   employee
GROUP BY TO_CHAR(start_date, 'YYYYMM')


YEAR_MON TOT_SALARY
-------- ----------
200905       5760
200910       3100
201409       3100
201709       2650
201801       2800
202003       2800
```

DB2 z/OS, DB2 LUW:

```
SELECT VARCHAR_FORMAT(start_date, 'YYYYMM')  AS year_mon,
              SUM(salary) AS tot_salary
FROM   employee
GROUP BY VARCHAR_FORMAT (start_date, 'YYYYMM')
```

SQL Server:

```
SELECT FORMAT (start_date, 'yyyyMM') AS year_mon,  -- upper M
              SUM(salary) AS tot_salary
FROM   employee
GROUP BY FORMAT (start_date, 'yyyyMM')
```

MySQL:

```
SELECT DATE_FORMAT (start_date, '%Y%m') AS year_mon,
              SUM(salary) AS tot_salary
FROM   employee
GROUP BY DATE_FORMAT (start_date, '%Y%m')
```

Hive:

```
SELECT DATE_FORMAT (start_date, 'yyyyMM') AS year_mon,
            SUM(salary) AS tot_salary
FROM   employee
GROUP BY FORMAT (start_date, 'yyyyMM')
```

If you want to maintain a summary table, add the INSERT clause as the first row like this:

```
INSERT INTO salary_summary (year_month, salary_sum)
SELECT TO_CHAR(start_date, 'YYYYMM')  AS year_mon,
            SUM(salary) AS tot_salary
FROM   employee
GROUP BY TO_CHAR(start_date, 'YYYYMM')
```

## 18.6 Calculating Age from Date of Birth

The topic of calculating the age of a person from the date of birth is seldom discussed, even though the need for this calculation is quite common. How should the age of somebody born on the 29th of February be calculated? That is, is the time between 29.2.2020 and 28.2.2021 one year?

The following examples show how to calculate the age. We will use start_date in the employee table to calculate the number of years of employment for each employee.

SQL Server:

```
SELECT lname, fname, start_date, GETDATE() AS today,
   (10000*Year(GETDATE())+100*Month(GETDATE())+Day(GETDATE()) -
(10000*Year(start_date)+100*Month(start_date)+Day(start_date)))
/10000  AS e_years
FROM employee
```

```
lname   fname  start_date               today                   e_years
------  ------ ------------------------ ------------------------ -------
Stream  Peter  2020-03-02 00:00:00.000  2024-10-17 16:42:09.850  4
Wood    Mike   2009-10-15 00:00:00.000  2024-10-17 16:42:09.850  15
Brooke  Rachel 2014-09-24 00:00:00.000  2024-10-17 16:42:09.850  10
Lake    Leon   2018-01-01 00:00:00.000  2024-10-17 16:42:09.850  6
Taylor  Peter  2009-05-12 00:00:00.000  2024-10-17 16:42:09.850  15
Brown   Laura  2017-09-15 00:00:00.000  2024-10-17 16:42:09.850  7
River   Lilian 2009-05-12 00:00:00.000  2024-10-17 16:42:09.850  15
```

SQL Server alternative:

```
SELECT lname, fname, start_date, GETDATE() AS today,
  YEAR(GETDATE()) - YEAR(start_date) -
   CASE
     WHEN FORMAT (GETDATE(),'MM-dd') < FORMAT(start_date
        ,'MM-dd') THEN 1 ELSE 0
     END AS e_years
FROM employee
```

The statement calculates the year difference which is then subtracted by 0 or 1. 0 if we have today already passed the month and 1 if not. If we have passed the month, then the year has elapsed and nothing is subtracted. If not, then one year is subtracted from the result.

DB2:

```
SELECT lname, fname, start_date, CURRENT_DATE AS today,
   YEAR (CURRENT_DATE - start_date) AS e_years
FROM employee
```

PostgreSQL:

```
SELECT lname, fname, start_date, CURRENT_DATE AS today,
      AGE(start_date) as e_years
FROM employee
```

Oracle :

```
SELECT lname, fname, start_date, SYSDATE AS today,
   FLOOR(MONTHS_BETWEEN (SYSDATE, start_date)/12) AS e_years
FROM employee
```

Here is an alternative that takes into consideration the leap year in a different way:

```
SELECT lname, fname, start_date, SYSDATE  AS today,
  TO_CHAR (SYSDATE, 'YYYY') - TO_CHAR(start_date, 'YYYY') -
    CASE
      WHEN TO_CHAR (SYSDATE, 'MMDD') < TO_CHAR(start_date,
                  'MMDD') THEN 1 ELSE 0
    END AS e_years
FROM employee
```

Snowflake:

```
SELECT lname, fname, start_date, CURRENT_DATE AS "today",
   FLOOR(MONTHS_BETWEEN (CURRENT_DATE, start_date)/12) AS
          e_years
FROM employee
```

MySQL:
```
SELECT lname, fname, start_date, CURRENT_DATE AS today,
  YEAR(CURRENT_DATE) - YEAR(start_date) -
    CASE
      WHEN FORMAT(CURRENT_DATE,'MM-dd') <   FORMAT(start_date
            ,'MM-dd')
      THEN 1 ELSE 0
      END AS e_years
FROM employee
```

Please test your statements. We do not guarantee that these age statements work in all circumstances.

---

## 18.7 Finding Duplicate Rows

When receiving data from external sources, the data often contains duplicate rows. We can spot the duplicates using SQL. The temporary table w_project has been erroneously populated in the following example with duplicate rows. No primary key was defined, so the system did not take care of eliminating duplicates. Now, we only want to fetch duplicates. The table w_project looks like this after we have loaded the data:

```
projno project_name     priority location
------ ------------     -------- ---------
P5     CUSTOMERS        3        SINGAPORE
P6     STATISTICS       NULL     NULL
P1     BOOKKEEPING      2        LONDON
P2     BILLING          1        HELSINKI
P6     STATISTICS       NULL     NULL
P3     WAREHOUSING      3        HELSINKI
P4     ACCOUNTING       2        LONDON
P5     CUSTOMERS        3        SINGAPORE
P6     STATISTICS       NULL     NULL
```

*Fetch all duplicates and their count from the table w_project.*

```
SELECT projno, project_name, priority, location, COUNT(*)AS cnt
FROM w_project
GROUP BY projno, project_name, priority, location
HAVING COUNT(*) > 1
```

| PROJNO | PROJECT_NAME | PRIORITY | LOCATION | CNT |
|--------|--------------|----------|----------|-----|
| P5 | CUSTOMERS | 3 | SINGAPORE | 2 |
| P6 | STATISTICS | NULL | NULL | 3 |

Think of a million-row table with one duplicate row. Well, the query above finds it!

Just to show another way, we use a subquery (this time without the count):

```
SELECT projno, project_name, priority, location
FROM w_project a
WHERE 1 <
   (SELECT COUNT(*)
    FROM w_project b
    WHERE a.projno = b.projno)
ORDER BY 1, 2, 3
```

| PROJNO | PROJECT_NAME | PRIORITY | LOCATION |
|--------|--------------|----------|----------|
| P5 | CUSTOMERS | 3 | SINGAPORE |
| P5 | CUSTOMERS | 3 | SINGAPORE |
| P6 | STATISTICS | | |
| P6 | STATISTICS | | |
| P6 | STATISTICS | | |

Sometimes, we might get rows with the same primary key, but in other respects, the rows differ. For this purpose, the w_project now looks like this:

```
PROJNO  PROJECT_NAME      PRIORITY   LOCATION
------  ---------------   --------   ---------------
P5      CUSTOMERS              1      NEW YORK
P6      STATISTICS            2      NULL
P1      BOOKKEEPING           2      LONDON
P2      BILLING               1      HELSINKI
P6      STATS                 1      LONDON
P3      WAREHOUSING           3      HELSINKI
P4      ACCOUNTING            2      LONDON
P5      CUSTOMERS             3      SINGAPORE
P6      STATS PROJ            3      NULL
```

In the SELECT below, first the subquery fetches the duplicate primary keys, and then the main query retrieves all other information related to them.

```
SELECT *
FROM w_project
WHERE projno IN
     (SELECT projno
      FROM w_project
      GROUP BY projno
      HAVING COUNT(*) > 1)
ORDER BY projno
```

```
PROJNO  PROJECT_NAME     PRIORITY   LOCATION
----    ---------------  --------   ---------------
P5      CUSTOMERS            1       NEW YORK
P5      CUSTOMERS            3       SINGAPORE
P6      STATISTICS          2       NULL
P6      STATS               1       LONDON
P6      STATS PROJ          3       NULL
```

The result shows all variants of the same projno.

## 18.8 Removing Duplicate Rows

Until now, we have just listed the duplicates. Removing them is surprisingly tricky. Set theory rules: you can't just remove one of the duplicates since the DELETE statement will remove all qualifying rows!

However, using the ROW_NUMBER function, we get a unique value for each row. Then, we can delete duplicates by deleting all but max values. This is also a good example of how to use the WITH clause (Common Table Expression, CTE). Here, we already use the subquery-as-a-table concept described in Chapter 19.1. We remove the duplicates from the original w_project table. To be sure that we find the right rows to delete, we first **look** at the rows. The following WITH structure (inline view) contains the row number.

```
WITH project_with_rownumber as
    (SELECT projno, project_name, priority, location,
     ROW_NUMBER() OVER(ORDER BY projno) AS rownumber
     FROM w_project)
SELECT * FROM project_with_rownumber
WHERE rownumber NOT IN
(SELECT r              --  max row number for duplicates
 FROM
    (SELECT projno, project_name, priority, location,
            MAX(rownumber) AS r
     FROM project_with_rownumber
     GROUP BY projno, project_name, priority, location) a
 )
```

| projno | project_name | priority | location | rownumber |
| ------- | ------------ | --------- | --------- | --------- |
| P5 | CUSTOMERS | 3 | SINGAPORE | 5 |
| P6 | STATISTICS | NULL | NULL | 7 |
| P6 | STATISTICS | NULL | NULL | 8 |

The result set seems to contain all duplicate rows. To delete them, we just change the SELCET to DELETE, and because all conditions are the same as in the previous query, we can confidently run the delete query knowing that only those three rows will be deleted.

```
WITH project_with_rownumber as
    (SELECT projno, project_name, priority, location,
     ROW_NUMBER() OVER(ORDER BY projno) AS rownumber
     FROM w_project)
DELETE FROM project_with_rownumber
WHERE rownumber NOT IN
 (SELECT r                    --  max row number for duplicates
  FROM
    (SELECT projno, project_name, priority, location,
            MAX(rownumber) AS r
     FROM project_with_rownumber
     GROUP BY projno, project_name, priority, location) a
 )

3 rows affected.
```

We deleted rows so that only one row remained of each duplicate. That is, the one with the maximum row number.

# Powerful Joins and Subqueries

## 19.1 A Subquery as a Table, Derived Table

In the FROM clause, you can put an entire subquery in parenthesis instead of giving a table name. This is called the derived table. There are many interesting use cases for this construct.

First, a simple example to demonstrate the principle:

```
SELECT *
FROM
     (SELECT city, SUM(salary) AS total
      FROM employee
      GROUP BY city) city_total

CITY            TOTAL
----------  ----------
HELSINKI          6060
SYDNEY            5450
LONDON            8700
```

A subquery in the FROM clause is like a temporary view, it will be calculated for the duration of the SELECT statement and the result will disappear after that. The subquery is resolved first. After that, the outer SELECT. The result of the subquery feeds into the upper query. In Oracle, a subquery like this is called an "In line view" and in DB2, it is called a "table expression". The derived table (subquery) must be given a name (here "city_total"), except in Oracle. This name is used like a table name.

Let's look at a more realistic example. We saw a similar query in Chapter 9.1. Simple subquery.

*Fetch employees with the lowest tax rate, name, and tax rate.*

```
SELECT e.lname, e.fname, e.tax_rate
FROM employee e JOIN
     (SELECT MIN(tax_rate) AS min_tax_rate
      FROM employee) mintax        -- derived table: mintax
  ON e.tax_rate = mintax.min_tax_rate
```

| LNAME | FNAME | TAX_RATE |
|-------|-------|----------|
| Stream | Peter | 22 |
| Brown | Laura | 22 |

The subquery in parenthesis is like a temporary view with the name "mintax". The name can be prefixed with the keyword AS. min_tax_rate is a column in table mintax. You can use a derived table construct just to examine how many rows a query would return. For instance, the following query:

```
SELECT d.deptname, e.empno, e.lname,
       p.project_name, p.projno, pe.hours_act
FROM department d
LEFT JOIN employee e
    ON (d.deptno = e.deptno)
LEFT JOIN proj_emp pe
    ON (e.empno = pe.empno)
LEFT JOIN project p
    ON (p.projno = pe.projno)
ORDER BY d.deptname, e.lname
```

We just embed the query in the FROM clause, give it a name (below q1) and calculate the number of rows with the top-level query.

```
SELECT COUNT(*) AS cnt
FROM
(
SELECT d.deptname, e.empno, e.lname,
        p.project_name, p.projno, pe.hours_act
FROM department d
LEFT JOIN employee e
    ON (d.deptno = e.deptno)
LEFT JOIN proj_emp pe
    ON (e.empno = pe.empno)
LEFT JOIN project p
    ON (p.projno = pe.projno)
) q1

      CNT
----------
       12
```

This kind of query is also useful if you want to measure wall clock time for alternative query formulations without looking at all the result rows. You always get one row, but the whole statement will be executed, so you get an idea of the execution time.

We present several other examples in this chapter of using derived tables.

**EXERCISES**

1. Take a look at this query from the Chapter 9.2 Subqueries/Correlated Subqueries:

```
SELECT lname, fname, city, salary
 FROM employee e1
 WHERE salary <=
     (SELECT AVG(salary)
      FROM employee e2
      WHERE e2.city = e1.city)
```

In the query, you cannot include the actual salary average in the result. Change it to include the city average in the result (Tip: use a join and subquery as a table, grouping).

## 19.2 A Subquery in the SELECT List

The SELECT list can include columns that get their values from subqueries correlated with the main query to create summary reports. I thank Lauri Pietarinen for this example.

*Fetch the department number, name, employee count, total salary, max priority of the department's projects, and the total of department employees project hours (with all corresponding values on the same row).*

```
SELECT
    deptno,    deptname,
     (SELECT COUNT(*)
      FROM employee e
      WHERE e.deptno = d.deptno ) AS emp_count,
     (SELECT SUM(salary)
      FROM employee e
      WHERE e.deptno = d.deptno ) AS tot_salary,
     (SELECT MAX(priority)
      FROM employee e
          JOIN proj_emp pe
             ON pe.empno = e.empno
          JOIN project p
             ON p.projno = pe.projno
      WHERE e.deptno = d.deptno ) AS max_prio,
      (SELECT sum(hours_act)
       FROM employee e JOIN proj_emp pe
          ON e.empno = pe.empno
       WHERE e.deptno = d.deptno) AS tot_hours
    FROM department d
    ORDER BY deptno
```

| DEPTNO | DEPTNAME | EMP_COUNT | TOT_SALARY | MAX_PRIO | TOT_HOURS |
|--------|----------|-----------|------------|----------|-----------|
| 1 | IT | 2 | 5750.00 | 2 | 900 |
| 2 | Economy | 0 | NULL | NULL | NULL |
| 3 | Research | 3 | 8400.00 | 2 | 1000 |
| 4 | Marketing | 1 | 100.00 | 3 | 1700 |

## 19.3 Outer Join – Some Deeper Analysis

An outer join that has conditions can be surprisingly complex and might result in wrong results, if you are not careful. Let's look at an example:

*Fetch all departments and their employees in London: deptno, deptname, lname, and city.*

```
SELECT d.deptno, d.deptname, e.lname, e.city    -- Wrong result!
FROM department d
LEFT JOIN employee e
      ON (d.deptno = e.deptno)
WHERE e.city = 'LONDON'
ORDER BY d.deptno, e.lname
```

| DEPTNO | DEPTNAME | LNAME | CITY |
|---|---|---|---|
| 1 | IT | Wood | LONDON |
| 3 | Research | Lake | LONDON |
| 3 | Research | Stream | LONDON |

The result does not contain the Economy or Marketing departments, even though outer join should result in at least one row for each department. The problem is in the execution order: the WHERE condition is enforced **after** the outer join and all rows where the city does not equal London are discarded. The intermediate result after the outer join looks like this:

| DEPTNO | DEPTNAME | LNAME | CITY |
|---|---|---|---|
| 1 | IT | Wood | LONDON |
| 1 | IT | Brown | SYDNEY |
| 2 | Economy | NULL | NULL |
| 3 | Research | River | SYDNEY |
| 3 | Research | Lake | LONDON |
| 3 | Research | Stream | LONDON |
| 4 | Marketing | Brooke | HELSINKI |

The city of department 2 is NULL (left outer join has generated the NULL value for the rows missing from the rightmost table). The intermediate result is then filtered by the condition WHERE city = 'LONDON' so that the Economy department is discarded, since its city is NULL. Hence, we get the wrong result.

We can fix the statement with a derived subquery:

```
SELECT d.deptno, d.deptname, e.lname, e.city
FROM department d
LEFT JOIN
  (SELECT * FROM employee
   WHERE city = 'LONDON') e
ON d.deptno = e.deptno
ORDER BY d.deptno, e.lname
```

| DEPTNO | DEPTNAME | LNAME | CITY |
|--------|----------|-------|------|
| 1 | IT | Wood | LONDON |
| 2 | Economy | NULL | NULL |
| 3 | Research | Lake | LONDON |
| 3 | Research | Stream | LONDON |
| 4 | Marketing | NULL | NULL |

Now, the subquery is executed first, so that only employees from London are left. Only then is the outer join executed, and all departments are included. We see all the departments and also that departments 2 and 4 have no employees from London. Another, perhaps more convenient way to obtain the correct result is to include the condition in the ON clause instead of the WHERE clause:

```
SELECT d.deptno, d.deptname, e.lname, e.city
FROM department d
LEFT JOIN employee e
  ON (d.deptno = e.deptno
  AND e.city = 'LONDON')
ORDER BY d.deptno, e.lname
```

Remember this rule for outer joins:

If the "child table" of an outer join (e.g. the right table in a LEFT JOIN) has conditions, use a subquery in FROM or move the conditions into the ON clause.

Another feature of the outer join is that the conditions in the ON clause will not restrict the final result. This is different from the WHERE clause, which does restrict the final results.

*Fetch the departments 'IT', 'Economy', and 'Marketing' together with their employees: deptno, deptname, last name, and city.*

```
SELECT d.deptno, d.deptname, e.lname, e.city
FROM department d
LEFT JOIN employee e
  ON (d.deptno = e.deptno
  AND d.deptname IN ('IT', 'Economy', 'Marketing'))
ORDER BY d.deptno, e.lname
```

| DEPTNO | DEPTNAME  | LNAME  | CITY     |
|-------:|-----------|--------|----------|
| 1 | IT        | Brown  | LONDON   |
| 1 | IT        | Wood   | LONDON   |
| 2 | Economy   | NULL   | NULL     |
| 3 | Research  | NULL   | NULL     |
| 4 | Marketing | Brooke | HELSINKI |

The safest way is the following:

```
SELECT d.deptno, d.deptname, e.lname, e.city
FROM department d
LEFT JOIN employee e
  ON (d.deptno = e.deptno)
WHERE d.deptname IN ('IT', 'Economy', 'Marketing')
ORDER BY d.deptno, e.lname
```

| DEPTNO | DEPTNAME | LNAME | CITY |
|--------|----------|-------|------|
| 1 | IT | Brown | LONDON |
| 1 | IT | Wood | LONDON |
| 2 | Economy | NULL | NULL |
| 4 | Marketing | Brooke | HELSINKI |

## EXERCISES

1.  Get all employees and show departments for those who work in Marketing or Research departments. All employees must appear in the result. Be careful if you have an AND and OR clause.

---

## 19.4 Cartesian product

Sometimes, we need a Cartesian product between two tables: each row in the first table is joined with every row in the second. First, we will use the traditional join syntax. Please note that we are doing a self-join (employee to employee) and intentionally leave out the join condition.

*Generate all possible combinations of employees.*

```
SELECT e1.empno, e1.lname, e1.fname,
    e2.empno, e2.lname, e2.fname
FROM employee e1, employee e2
```

| EMPNO | LNAME | FNAME | EMPNO | LNAME | FNAME |
|-------|-------|-------|-------|-------|-------|
| 2134 | Stream | Peter | 2134 | Stream | Peter |
| 2134 | Stream | Peter | 2234 | Wood | Mike |
| 2134 | Stream | Peter | 2245 | Brooke | Rachel |
| 2134 | Stream | Peter | 2345 | Lake | Leon |
| 2134 | Stream | Peter | 2884 | Taylor | Peter |
| 2134 | Stream | Peter | 3546 | Brown | Laura |
| 2134 | Stream | Peter | 3547 | River | Lilian |
| 2234 | Wood | Mike | 2134 | Stream | Peter |
| 2234 | Wood | Mike | 2234 | Wood | Mike |
| 2234 | Wood | Mike | 2245 | Brooke | Rachel |
| 2234 | Wood | Mike | 2345 | Lake | Leon |
| 2234 | Wood | Mike | 2884 | Taylor | Peter |
| 2234 | Wood | Mike | 3546 | Brown | Laura |
| 2234 | Wood | Mike | 3547 | River | Lilian |
| 2245 | Brooke | Rachel | 2134 | Stream | Peter |
| 2245 | Brooke | Rachel | 2234 | Wood | Mike |
| 2245 | Brooke | Rachel | 2245 | Brooke | Rachel |

...

There are 49 rows in total (7x7). The end of the result has been cut off to save space. The order of the rows might differ, because it is unspecified. How would you prevent pairing of the same employee (Stream – Stream)?

Using the Join syntax, the same result is obtained like this:

```
SELECT e1.empno, e1.lname, e1.fname,
    e2.empno, e2.lname, e2.fname
FROM employee e1
    CROSS JOIN  employee e2
```

In this case, the ON clause is not used.

## 19.5 Division – All Included

By division, we mean a "get those x, that include all y". SQL does not have such an operation directly, but you can do it using the EXISTS operator. See example below:

*Find all those projects that all employees belong to.*

```
SELECT project_name
FROM project p
WHERE NOT EXISTS
        (SELECT *
         FROM employee e
         WHERE NOT EXISTS
             (SELECT *
              FROM proj_emp pe
              WHERE pe.projno = p.projno
              AND pe.empno = e.empno))


PROJECT_NAME
----------------
BOOKKEEPING
```

Verbally, the solution could be described like this: Get the project names for all projects for which there doesn't exist an employee that doesn't belong to the project. If no such employee exists, then all belong. The SQL guru Joe Celko illustrates this with a small example: "Imagine a World War II movie where a cocky pilot has just walked into the hangar, looked over the fleet, and announced, 'There ain't no plane in this hangar that I can't fly!'"

In the query on the facing page, we compare the total number of employees with the number of employees in a specific project. If they are the same, we can reason that all employees must belong to the project.

```
SELECT project_name FROM project
WHERE projno IN
   (SELECT projno
    FROM proj_emp
    GROUP BY projno
    HAVING COUNT(empno) =
        (SELECT COUNT(*)
         FROM employee))
```

## 19.6 ANY and ALL Subqueries

ANY and ALL operators are seldom used.

If we need a comparison operator other than equal (for instance, > or <) when checking values from subqueries, we can't use IN. Instead, we must use one of ANY, SOME, or ALL together with the comparison operator.

```
ANY       if any of the values from the subquery fulfills the
          condition
SOME      same as ANY
ALL       if each and every one of the values fulfills the
          condition
```

ANY and ALL operators can be defined in the following way:

X is a column and OP is a comparison operator (for instance >, < or >= ) and {a, b, ... , h} is the set of values produced by the subquery.

```
*X OP ANY {a,b,  ... , h} is the same as
X OP a OR X OP b OR ... OR X OP h
*X OP ALL {a,b,  ... , h} is the same as
X OP a AND X OP b AND ... AND X OP h
```

Let's look at some examples:

*Which employees have a higher salary than all employees from Sydney?*

```
SELECT lname, city, salary
FROM employee
WHERE salary > ALL
      (SELECT salary
       FROM employee
       WHERE city = 'SYDNEY')
```

```
LNAME      CITY          SALARY
-------    ---------     --------
Wood       LONDON        3100
Brooke     HELSINKI      3100
Taylor     HELSINKI      2960
```

The subquery produces an intermediate set of values {2650, 2800}. The main query selects all employees whose salary is greater than all salaries in the set.

Chapter 19.9 contains a useful example of using ALL.

*Fetch all employees whose tax rate is 31 or more, except for the employee with the highest salary.*

```
SELECT lname, salary, tax_rate
FROM employee
WHERE tax_rate >= 31
AND salary < ANY
      (SELECT salary
       FROM employee)
```

```
LNAME         SALARY     TAX_RATE
----------    ----------  ----------
Taylor         2960          31
River          2800          37
```

Simply stated, all other employees have a salary less than at least one of these salaries, except for the employee with the highest salary. The subquery produces a temporary result set

{2800, 3100, 3100, 2800, 2960, 2650, 2800}. The main query retrieves those whose salaries are less than at least one of these.

The same result can, of course, be obtained using the max function:

```
SELECT lname, salary, tax_rate
FROM employee
WHERE tax_rate >= 31
AND salary <>
    (SELECT MAX(salary)
     FROM employee)
```

## 19.7 Comparing Tables

Sometimes, in the context of data warehousing and ETL/ELT loading or database testing, you need to compare the contents of two tables (with the same structure) and find out:

- Which rows are new
- Which rows have been removed
- Which rows have been changed

This kind of comparison is needed when you are updating a dimension in a star schema, or a satellite in the Data Vault method.

Let's say we have a table employee in the data warehouse whose data needs to be refreshed from the operational system. That is, there have been updates in the operational system since the previous data warehouse load. We have created a worktable employee_w, into which the current, fresh employee data from the operational system is copied. The rows of the tables employee_w and employee differ somewhat from each other.

Let's take a look at what employee_w looks like (to save space, only a subset of the columns are shown).

```
SELECT empno, lname, fname, education, salary, start_date
FROM employee_w

EMPNO LNAME       FNAME       EDUCATION    SALARY START_DATE
----  ----------  ----------  -----------  ------ ----------
2134  Stream      Peter       Ba             2800 2020-03-02
2234  Wood        Mike        PhD            3100 2009-10-15
2245  Brooke      Rachel      MS             3100 2014-09-24
2884  Taylor      Peter       MA             2960 2009-05-12
3546  Brown       Laura       Ba             2750 2017-09-15
3547  River       Lilian      DIP            2800 2009-05-12
2346  Stone       Roger       NULL           2800 2018-01-01
2347  Meadow      Melissa     NULL           2900 2020-10-15
```

First, let's find the new rows. That is, employees, that are in the employee_w table but not in the employee table. employee_w is the "new" table and employee is the "old" table:

```
SELECT new.empno, new.lname, new.fname, new.education,
       new.salary, new.start_date
FROM employee_w new
LEFT JOIN employee old
   ON (new.empno = old.empno)
WHERE old.empno IS NULL

EMPNO LNAME       FNAME       EDUCATION   SALARY START_DATE
----  ----------  ----------  ---------  ---------- ----------
2346 Stone        Roger       NULL           2800 2018-01-01
2347 Meadow       Melissa     NULL           2900 2020-10-15
```

Then, the removed rows, that is, rows that are in employee (old) but not in the new employee_w (new), have been deleted from the operational system.

```
SELECT old.empno, old.lname, old.fname, old.education,
       old.salary, old.start_date
FROM employee_w new
RIGHT JOIN employee old
    ON (new.empno = old.empno)
WHERE new.empno IS NULL
```

| EMPNO | LNAME | FNAME | EDUCATION | SALARY | START_DATE |
|-------|-------|-------|-----------|--------|------------|
| 2345  | Lake  | Leon  |           | 2800   | 2018-01-01 |

Finally, all rows that have changed. That is, the empno is the same but some other value has been changed in the operational system (note that to save space, only a subset of the columns are shown):

```
SELECT new.empno, new.lname, new.fname, new.education,
       new.salary, new.start_date
FROM employee_w new
JOIN employee old
    ON (new.empno = old.empno)
WHERE new.lname <> old.lname
OR new.fname <> old.fname
OR new.education <> old.education
OR new.salary <> old.salary
OR new.start_date <> old.start_date
```

| EMPNO | LNAME  | FNAME  | EDUCATION | SALARY | START_DATE |
|-------|--------|--------|-----------|--------|------------|
| 2245  | Brooke | Rachel | MS        | 3100   | 2014-09-24 |
| 3546  | Brown  | Laura  | Ba        | 2750   | 2017-09-15 |

The rows in the result set have changed for one or several columns, and that change must be processed into the data warehouse.

The NULLs might cause problems because one NULL is not equal to another NULL. So, new columns with NULL will be evaluated not equal, even when no actual change has been taken place. You should use the COALESCE function for all comparison columns, for instance:

```
COALESCE (new.education, ' ') <> COALESCE(old.education, ' ')
```

and for numeric columns:

```
COALESCE (new.salary,-10)  <> COALESCE (old.salary,-10).
```

For numeric columns, use, for instance, -10 as a replacement for NULL, as above. Remember that the value you choose must not be present in the data. So, if old and new values are both NULL, they will be set to -10, which means no change.

You can also use the ANSI standard IS DISTINCT FROM in DB2, PostgreSQL, SQL Server, and Snowflake. Write it like this:

```
new.education IS DISTINCT FROM old.education
```

The expression results in TRUE even when both sides are NULL. It is NULL-safe.

You could also compare all columns in one go by using a hash function. That could speed up the query a lot if the tables are big. In this method, you concatenate all columns and put them into a hash function. In MySQL and PostgreSQL, the hash function is MD5(). In SQL Server, use HASHBYTES().

These queries are quite fast. Another method to search for new and removed rows is a NOT EXISTS subquery (see Page 135 EXISTS).

---

## 19.8 Handling Hierarchies and Self Joins

We introduce a new table, employee2, to demonstrate how hierarchies are handled. Each row has a reference to the employee's superior. The foreign key column 'boss' refers to the empno of the superior. The column 'level' shows the level of the hierarchy, 1 being the highest level. Below, you can see the structure and the rows of employee2.

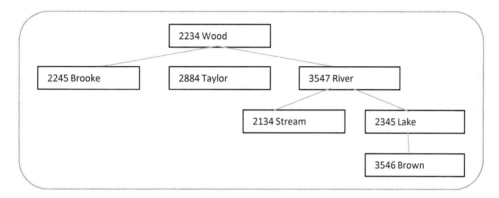

Figure 20: Hierarchy of employee2.

| EMPNO | FNAME | LNAME | CITY | EDUCATION | SALARY | BOSS | LEVEL |
|-------|-------|-------|------|-----------|--------|------|-------|
| 2234 | Mike | Wood | LONDON | PhD | 3100 | NULL | 1 |
| 2245 | Rachel | Brooke | HELSINKI | MA | 3100 | 2234 | 2 |
| 3547 | Lilian | River | SYDNEY | DIP | 2800 | 2234 | 2 |
| 2884 | Peter | Taylor | HELSINKI | MA | 2960 | 2234 | 2 |
| 2134 | Peter | Stream | LONDON | Ba | 2800 | 3547 | 3 |
| 2345 | Leon | Lake | LONDON | NULL | 2800 | 3547 | 3 |
| 3546 | Laura | Brown | SYDNEY | Ba | 2650 | 2345 | 4 |

To obtain a report with the organization structure, we must make a **self-join**. Our report has the data of the boss and his/her subordinate on the same row. It is helpful to think that we have two identical tables. That is, boss and subordinate. The "tables" are joined using the columns empno in boss (primary key) and bossno in subordinate (foreign key).

```
SELECT boss.empno AS boss, boss.lname AS boss_lname,
       boss.fname AS boss_fname, boss.level AS boss_level,
       subordinate.empno, subordinate.lname, subordinate.fname,
       subordinate.level
FROM employee2 boss
JOIN employee2 subordinate
     ON subordinate.boss = boss.empno
ORDER BY boss.level
```

| BOSS | BOSS_LNAME | BOSS_FNAME | BOSS_LEVEL | EMPNO | LNAME | FNAME | LEVEL |
| ---- | ---------- | ---------- | ---------- | ----- | ------ | --------- | ----- |
| 2234 | Wood | Mike | 1 | 2245 | Brook | Rachel | 2 |
| 2234 | Wood | Mike | 1 | 2884 | Taylor | Peter | 2 |
| 2234 | Wood | Mike | 1 | 3547 | River | Lilian | 2 |
| 3547 | River | Lilian | 2 | 2134 | Stream | Peter | 3 |
| 3547 | River | Lilian | 2 | 2345 | Lake | Leon | 3 |
| 2345 | Lake | Leon | 3 | 3546 | Brown | Laura | 4 |

We were able to run this query because table employee2 contains a column called "level". If that column hadn't existed, the result would have been confusing because we wouldn't have been able to sort it.

The ANSI standard extends the SQL SELECT statement with the Common Table Expression (CTE). Starting with the WITH keyword, we can define a temporary table that is referenced by the UNION ALL construct. This construct allows us to formulate recursive queries to handle hierarchical data.

In the example below, we generate the 'level' column on the fly.

```
WITH hierarchy (level, boss, bname, empno, lname, fname) AS
  (
   SELECT 1 as level, h1.boss,h2.lname,
          h1. empno, h1.lname, h1.fname
   FROM employee2 h1, employee2 h2
   WHERE h1.boss = '2234'
   AND h1.boss = h2.empno
   UNION ALL
   SELECT hier.level + 1 as level, e.boss,
          hier.lname, e.empno, e.lname, e.fname
   FROM employee2 emp, hierarchy hier
   WHERE e.boss = hier.empno
   )
SELECT boss, bname, empno, lname, fname, level
FROM hierarchy
```

| boss | bname | empno | lname | fname | level |
| ------- | ----- | ---- | ------- | ----- | ----- |
| 2234 | Wood | 2245 | Brooke | Rachel | 1 |
| 2234 | Wood | 2884 | Taylor | Peter | 1 |
| 2234 | Wood | 3547 | River | Lilian | 1 |
| 3547 | River | 2134 | Stream | Peter | 2 |
| 3547 | River | 2345 | Lake | Leon | 2 |
| 2345 | Lake | 3546 | Brown | Laura | 3 |

Oracle has a proprietary syntax for handling hierarchies, which is here briefly introduced. This query will show the hierarchy. The top level is the starting point.

```
SELECT boss, empno, lname, fname
FROM employee2
START WITH empno = '2234'
CONNECT BY boss = PRIOR empno


BOSS EMPNO LNAME        FNAME
---- ----  ----------   ----------
     2234  Wood         Mike
2234 2245  Brooke       Rachel
2234 2884  Taylor       Peter
2234 3547  River        Lilian
3547 2134  Stream       Peter
3547 2345  Lake         Leopold
2345 3546  Brown        Laura
```

---

## 19.9 "Most of" Queries

Getting the most common values of a column is surprisingly complex. For instance:

*Which locations have the most projects?*

```
SELECT location, COUNT(*) AS cnt
FROM project
GROUP BY location
HAVING COUNT(*) >= ALL
       (SELECT COUNT(*)
        FROM project
        GROUP BY location)


LOCATION               CNT
---------------  ----------
HELSINKI                 2
LONDON                   2
```

The subquery fetches the number of projects in different locations and produces an intermediate result set {1,2,1,2}. The main query runs through the locations and chooses those whose count is greater or equal to all the values in the result set. We end up with two locations with the most projects. We can get the same result by using a derived table (Subquery as a table):

```
SELECT location, cnt
FROM
    (SELECT location, COUNT(*) AS cnt
     FROM project
     GROUP BY location) s1
WHERE cnt =
        (SELECT MAX(location_cnt)
         FROM
                (SELECT location, COUNT(*) AS location_cnt
                 FROM project
                 GROUP BY location
                 ) s2
          )
```

We can simplify the query considerably by using a common table expression (CTE), where we first define the grouping query and then reuse the definition. This way, we don't have to repeat the subquery.

```
WITH location_cnt
AS
   (SELECT location,  COUNT(*) AS cnt
    FROM project
    GROUP BY location)
SELECT location, cnt
FROM location_cnt
WHERE cnt =
       (SELECT MAX(cnt)
        FROM location_cnt)
```

First, the query location_count is defined, and then it is used in the final query.

## EXERCISES

1. Find the cities with the most employees (employee table). Columns city and cnt.

## 19.10 At Most n or None

Fetch projects with at most two employees:

```
SELECT projno, project_name
FROM project
WHERE projno IN
    (SELECT projno
     FROM proj_emp
     GROUP BY projno
     HAVING COUNT(*) <= 2)


PROJNO PROJECT_NAME
------ ---------------
P2     BILLING
P3     WAREHOUSING
```

Projects P2 and P3 are in the result, which is fine, but we are missing projects P5 and P6 which have no employees! This query fixes the problem:

```
SELECT projno, project_name
FROM project p
WHERE NOT EXISTS
    (SELECT projno
     FROM proj_emp pe
     WHERE pe.projno = p.projno
     GROUP BY projno
     HAVING COUNT(*) > 2)


PROJNO PROJECT_NAME
------ ---------------
P2     BILLING
P3     WAREHOUSING
P5     CUSTOMERS
P6     STATISTICS
```

Here is another formulation which brings the same result:

```
SELECT projno, project_name
FROM project
WHERE 2 >=
    (SELECT COUNT(*)
     FROM proj_emp
     WHERE proj_emp.projno = project.projno)
```

## 19.11 Replacing a Correlated Subquery with a Derived Table

In the chapter on correlated subqueries, there was an example where we fetched the highest earners for each city. The same can be done using a derived table (subquery in the FROM clause), a solution that might be easier to understand. Please note the two-part join condition in the ON clause:

```
SELECT h1.city, h1.salary, h1.lname
FROM employee h1
JOIN
    (SELECT city, MAX(salary) max_salary
     FROM employee
     GROUP BY city) h2
    ON (h1.city = h2.city
    AND h1.salary = h2.max_salary)
ORDER BY h1.city

CITY            SALARY LNAME
----------  ---------- ------
HELSINKI          3100 Brooke
LONDON            3100 Wood
SYDNEY            2800 River
```

Here is the same query using the traditional syntax:

```
SELECT h1.city, h1.salary, h1.lname
FROM employee h1,
   (SELECT city, MAX(salary) AS max_salary
    FROM employee
    GROUP BY city) h2
WHERE h2.city = h1.city
AND h1.salary = h2.max_salary
ORDER BY h1.city
```

---

## 19.12 Building a Star Schema Join

Star schemas are popular in data warehouse solutions, often in the presentation layer, to support business intelligence tools. The method is also called dimensional modeling. A star schema model includes several dimension tables and one fact table.

Build the star schema join by starting with the fact table. In that way, the order of tables in the join will go right.

Here is a schematic command structure:

```
SELECT dim1.col2, dim1.col3, dim2.col2, dim2.col4, f.col5, …
FROM fact_table f
    JOIN dimension1 dim1
       ON (dim1.col1 = f.col1)
    JOIN dimension2 dim2
       ON (dim2.col1 = f.col2)
    JOIN dimension3 dim3
       ON (dim3 = f.col3)
    JOIN dimension4 dim4
       ON (dim4 = f.dim4)
    …
    WHERE …
```

# CHAPTER TWENTY

# Analytical and Statistical Queries

## 20.1 Statistical Functions

*Standard Deviation, Variance, and Standard Error*

The statistics standard deviation variance and standard error of the mean can be obtained with the functions STDDEV, VARIANCE, and SQRT, which are aggregate functions like MIN, MAX, COUNT, AVG, and SUM. In SQL Server, use STDEV instead of STDDEV and VAR instead of VARIANCE.

```
SELECT STDDEV(salary) AS std_dev,
       VARIANCE(salary) AS salary_var,
       STDDEV(salary)/SQRT(COUNT(*)) AS mean_error
FROM employee

STD_DEV    SALARY_VAR   MEAN_ERROR
---------- ------------ -----------
170.754627 29157.142857 64.53918284
```

## Median and Mode

The median is the value that is "in the middle". That is, there are an equal number of smaller and larger values. The following statement calculates the median of the salaries.

```
SELECT e1.salary AS median
FROM employee e1, employee e2
GROUP BY e1.salary
HAVING
    SUM(CASE WHEN e2.salary <= e1.salary THEN 1
             ELSE 0
         END) >= (COUNT(*)+1)/2
AND
    SUM(CASE WHEN e2.salary >= e1.salary THEN 1
             ELSE 0
         END) >= (COUNT(*)/2)+1


MEDIAN
------
   2800
```

The mode is the most common, that is, the most probable value.

*Find the most common salary.*

SQL Server:
```
SELECT TOP 1 *
FROM
   (SELECT salary AS mode_s, COUNT(*) AS cnt
    FROM employee
    GROUP BY salary
    ) A
 ORDER BY cnt DESC


mode_s    cnt
--------  ---
2800.00    3
```

Snowflake, MySQL, PostgreSQL, and Hive:

```
SELECT *
FROM
  (SELECT salary AS mode_s, COUNT(*) AS cnt
   FROM employee
   GROUP BY salary
     ) A
ORDER BY cnt DESC
LIMIT 1
```

DB2, PostgreSQL, Snowflake, and Oracle:

```
SELECT *
FROM
  (SELECT salary AS mode_s, COUNT(*) AS cnt
   FROM employee
   GROUP BY salary
     ) A
ORDER BY cnt DESC
FETCH FIRST 1 ROWS ONLY
```

## Distribution

We can calculate the value distribution of a given column. That is, what different values are in a column and how many of each value are there? We want to see both numbers and percentages for each different value.

*Fetch the distribution of the values of the city column and the percentage share of each value of the total, most common values first.*

```
SELECT e.city, COUNT(*) AS cnt,
    COUNT(*) * 100.0/j.emp_total_cnt AS share_perc
FROM employee e
CROSS JOIN
  (SELECT COUNT(*) AS emp_total_cnt
   FROM employee) j
GROUP BY e.city, j.emp_total_cnt
ORDER BY cnt DESC

city      cnt  share_perc
-------   ---  ----------------
LONDON    3    42.857142857142
SYDNEY    2    28.571428571428
HELSINKI  2    28.571428571428
```

The join uses the CROSS JOIN format. The total amount of employees (7), emp_total_cnt, calculated in the subquery is combined with every row so that we can calculate the percentage. Because COUNT(*) and j.emp_cnt are integer numbers, the result is also integer, cutting decimals away. The trick is to put 100.0 instead of 100 to get a decimal as the result. Note that j.emp_total_cnt must also be in the GROUP BY clause.

You can use the ROUND function to shorten the decimal part, which is the beginning of the query:

```
SELECT e.city, COUNT(*) AS cnt,
    ROUND(COUNT(*) * 100.0/j.emp_total_cnt, 2) AS share_perc
```

In SQL Server, the ROUND function does not cut the decimals nicely, so use CAST instead and convert to DECIMAL (5, 2).

This is another way to write the same query:

```
SELECT city, COUNT(*) AS cnt,
    COUNT(*) * 100.0/
            (SELECT COUNT(*)
            FROM employee) AS share_perc
FROM employee
GROUP BY city
ORDER BY cnt DESC
```

A subquery in the SELECT list is used to calculate the total number of employees.

Distribution queries are handy if you want to evaluate data quality in a table. For example, if you have a gender code, with this type of a query you can find the percentage of all different values in that column, including blanks, NULLS, and other errors. Quality queries like this are called data profiling queries.

## 20.2 Cumulative Sum

The cumulative sum is easy to add to the list of columns with the following subquery.

*Fetch employees and their salaries so that the cum_salary column grows cumulatively:*

```
SELECT lname, salary,
       (SELECT SUM(salary)
        FROM employee e1
        WHERE e1.empno <= e2.empno) AS cum_salary
FROM employee e2
ORDER BY e2.empno
```

| EMPNO | LNAME  | FNAME  | SALARY | CUM_SALARY |
|-------|--------|--------|--------|------------|
| 2134  | Stream | Peter  | 2800   | 2800       |
| 2234  | Wood   | Mike   | 3100   | 5900       |
| 2245  | Brooke | Rachel | 3100   | 9000       |
| 2345  | Lake   | Leon   | 2800   | 11800      |
| 2884  | Taylor | Peter  | 2960   | 14760      |
| 3546  | Brown  | Laura  | 2650   | 17410      |
| 3547  | River  | Lilian | 2800   | 20210      |

The problem is that each subquery can return only one column. If we need several columns (e.g., sum and average), we can use the new analytical functions available in the SQL99 standard. We can also add the row number as a column.

```
SELECT empno, lname, fname, salary,
       SUM(salary)  OVER(ORDER BY empno) AS cum_salary,
       ROW_NUMBER() OVER(ORDER BY empno) AS rownumber
FROM employee
ORDER BY empno
```

| empno | lname  | fname  | salary  | cum_salary | rownumber |
|-------|--------|--------|---------|------------|-----------|
| 2134  | Stream | Peter  | 2800.00 | 2800.00    | 1         |
| 2234  | Wood   | Mike   | 3100.00 | 5900.00    | 2         |
| 2245  | Brooke | Rachel | 3100.00 | 9000.00    | 3         |
| 2345  | Lake   | Leon   | 2800.00 | 11800.00   | 4         |
| 2884  | Taylor | Peter  | 2960.00 | 14760.00   | 5         |
| 3546  | Brown  | Laura  | 2650.00 | 17410.00   | 6         |
| 3547  | River  | Lilian | 2800.00 | 20210.00   | 7         |

## 20.3 Grouping without GROUP BY

The following example shows a handy way to create a grouped result without using GROUP BY and a join by using a subquery in the SELECT clause. Please note that we can create only one column per subquery; see COUNT(*) below. The statement first reads a row for an employee and then calculates the number of projects for that employee. Then, each subsequent employee is read.

*Fetch the number of projects per employee: last name, first name, city, and number of projects.*

```
SELECT lname, fname, city,
    (SELECT COUNT(*) AS cnt
     FROM proj_emp pe
     WHERE pe.empno = e.empno) AS proj_cnt
FROM employee e
ORDER BY proj_cnt
```

| LNAME | FNAME | CITY | PROJ_CNT |
| --- | --- | --- | --- |
| Lake | Leon | LONDON | 1 |
| Brown | Laura | SYDNEY | 1 |
| River | Lilian | SYDNEY | 1 |
| Stream | Peter | LONDON | 2 |
| Wood | Mike | LONDON | 2 |
| Taylor | Peter | HELSINKI | 2 |
| Brooke | Rachel | HELSINKI | 4 |

Same result obtained by using GROUP BY and JOIN:

```
SELECT e.lname, e.fname, e.city, COUNT(*) AS proj_cnt
FROM employee e
JOIN proj_emp pe
    ON (pe.empno = e.empno )
GROUP BY e.lname, e.fname, e.city
ORDER BY proj_cnt
```

## 20.4 Grouping Salaries in Categories

Employees are to be divided into categories according to their salaries:

- category 1: employees whose salary is less than or equal to 2800
- category 2: employees whose salary is between 2801 and 3000
- category 3: employees whose salary is more than 3000

The following example shows how to make the division into categories using UNION.

```
SELECT  1 AS cat,  lname, salary
FROM employee
WHERE salary BETWEEN 0 AND 2800
UNION
SELECT 2, lname, salary
FROM employee
WHERE salary BETWEEN 2801 AND 3000
UNION
SELECT 3 , lname , salary
FROM employee
WHERE salary > 3000  ORDER BY 1,3
```

```
     CAT LNAME              SALARY
---------- ---------- ----------
       1 Brown              2650
       1 River              2800
       1 Stream             2800
       2 Lake               2800
       2 Taylor             2960
       3 Brooke             3100
       3 Wood               3100
```

The same result can be obtained by creating a table category, into which the min and max salaries for each category are saved:

| cat | mini_salary | max_salary |
|---|---|---|
| 1 | 0 | 2800 |
| 2 | 2081 | 3000 |
| 3 | 3001 | 99999 |

By joining the employee table to the category table, we get the same result:

```
SELECT c.cat, e.lname, e.salary
FROM employee e, category c
WHERE e.salary BETWEEN c.min_salary AND c.max_salary
ORDER BY c.cat, e.lname
```

The advantage of this solution is that it is now easier to add new categories or change existing ones.

## 20.5 Fetch Top n

A "Get top 10 customers" type of query is a common requirement.

*Four top earners:*

SQL Server, Snowflake:

```
SELECT TOP 4 lname, fname, salary
FROM employee
ORDER BY salary DESC
```

```
LNAME        FNAME           SALARY
----------   ----------   ----------
Wood         Mike            3100
Brooke       Rachel          3100
Taylor       Peter           2960
Stream       Peter           2800
```

DB2, Snowflake, PostgreSQL, Oracle:

```
SELECT lname, fname, salary
FROM employee
ORDER BY salary DESC
FETCH FIRST 4 ROWS ONLY
```

Snowflake, MySQL, PostgreSQL and Hive:

```
SELECT lname, fname, salary
FROM employee
ORDER BY salary DESC
LIMIT 4
```

The alternative is to use SQL analytical functions and get the ordinal number for each row with the same query:

```
SELECT *
FROM
   (SELECT lname, fname, salary,
          DENSE_RANK () OVER (ORDER BY salary DESC ) AS ord
     FROM employee) S
FETCH FIRST 4 ROWS ONLY   -- MySQL, PostgreSQL, Hive: LIMIT 4
```

Another requirement is that instead of restricting the number of rows to a certain fixed amount (as in the example above), we want all rows whose column value is within the top n values, so we don't know beforehand the exact number of rows in the result.

*Fetch employees that belong to the group of the top two earners (there can be more than two employees in the result).*

```
SELECT *
FROM
    (SELECT lname, fname, salary,
     DENSE_RANK() OVER (ORDER BY salary DESC ) AS ord
     FROM employee) s
WHERE s.ord < 3
```

| LNAME  | FNAME  | SALARY | ORD |
| ------ | ------ | ------ | --- |
| Wood   | Mike   | 3100   | 1   |
| Brooke | Rachel | 3100   | 1   |
| Taylor | Peter  | 2960   | 2   |

## EXERCISES

1. Get the three employees with the highest tax rates: lname, fname, and tax_rate.

2. Retrieve the employees whose tax rate is within the three highest tax rates.

## 20.6 Samples: Fetch Every Tenth Row

Sometimes, we need a random sample of the rows of a table, for instance, every tenth row. From our small employee table, we select every third row. The result can then be inserted into another table with the INSERT SELECT structure, if needed.

```
SELECT empno, lname, fname, city, salary
FROM (SELECT  empno, lname, fname, city, salary,
        ROW_NUMBER() OVER(ORDER BY empno) AS j
      FROM  employee) A1
WHERE (j - 1) = (FLOOR((j - 1) / 3)) * 3
```

| EMPNO | LNAME | FNAME | CITY | SALARY |
|-------|-------|-------|------|--------|
| 2134 | Stream | Peter | LONDON | 2800 |
| 2345 | Lake | Leon | LONDON | 2800 |
| 3547 | River | Lilian | SYDNEY | 2800 |

When searching for those whose sequence number j is the same as division by three, rounded down, and multiplied by three, we get every third. Instead of j, the expression j - 1 is used so that the first row is selected immediately.

You could also use the MOD function, then the last row would be:

```
WHERE MOD(j, 3) = 1   -- gives the reminder of j/3.
```

In SQL Server:

```
WHERE j%3 = 1   -- gives the reminder of j/3
```

---

### 20.7 Rankings, Partitions, Values from Previous on Next Row

The SQL2003 standard introduced functions for calculating the rank in the result. They belong to the so-called Window functions in SQL. Note that MySQL supports Windows functions starting from version 8.0.

*Rank employees by salary:*

```
SELECT lname, salary,
  RANK() OVER (ORDER BY salary DESC) AS ranking,
  DENSE_RANK () OVER (ORDER BY salary DESC) AS denserank,
  ROW_NUMBER () OVER (ORDER BY salary DESC) AS rownumber
FROM employee
```

| LNAME | SALARY | RANKING | DENSERANK | ROWNUMBER |
|---|---|---|---|---|
| Wood | 3100 | 1 | 1 | 1 |
| Brooke | 3100 | 1 | 1 | 2 |
| Taylor | 2960 | 3 | 2 | 3 |
| Stream | 2800 | 4 | 3 | 4 |
| River | 2800 | 4 | 3 | 5 |
| Lake | 2800 | 4 | 3 | 6 |
| Brown | 2650 | 7 | 4 | 7 |

*Rank employees by salary within each city separately.* This can be done with the PARTITION keyword.

```
SELECT lname, fname, salary,
  RANK() OVER (PARTITION BY city ORDER BY salary DESC) AS nr,
  city
FROM employee
ORDER BY city, salary DESC
```

| LNAME | FNAME | SALARY | NR | CITY |
|---|---|---|---|---|
| Brooke | Rachel | 3100 | 1 | HELSINKI |
| Taylor | Peter | 2960 | 2 | HELSINKI |
| Wood | Mike | 3100 | 1 | LONDON |
| Stream | Peter | 2800 | 2 | LONDON |
| Lake | Leon | 2800 | 2 | LONDON |
| River | Lilian | 2800 | 1 | SYDNEY |
| Brown | Laura | 2650 | 2 | SYDNEY |

*List employees with tax_rates. We also want to compare the tax_rate to the average tax_rate of each city.*

```
SELECT lname, fname, city, tax_rate,
       AVG(tax_rate) OVER (PARTITION BY city) AS city_avg
FROM employee
ORDER BY city, lname

lname      fname   city       tax_rate  city_avg
------     ------  --------    --------  ---------
Brooke     Rachel  HELSINKI    31.0      31.000000
Taylor     Peter   HELSINKI    31.0      31.000000
Lake       Leon    LONDON      24.5      26.500000
Stream     Peter   LONDON      22.0      26.500000
Wood       Mike    LONDON      33.0      26.500000
Brown      Laura   SYDNEY      22.0      29.500000
River      Lilian  SYDNEY      37.0      29.500000
```

NTILE is another Window function. We can select only, for instance, 50% of the table rows using it. For instance, NTILE(2) divides the result set into two groups with the same amount of rows. The groups will get a value of 1 or 2.

*Fetch 50% of employee table rows based on salary.*

```
SELECT *
FROM
(SELECT empno, lname, fname, salary,
     NTILE(2) OVER (ORDER BY salary ) AS ntile
  FROM employee) q
WHERE ntile = 1

empno  lname   fname   salary   ntile
-----  ------  ------  -------  -----
3546   Brown   Laura   2650.00  1
3547   River   Lilian  2800.00  1
2134   Stream  Peter   2800.00  1
2345   Lake    Leon    2800.00  1
```

Using the LAG and LEAD functions, you can search for the previous or next rows in a result set. This allows you to compare a row to the previous row or the next row, for example. The offset tells you how many rows are being searched compared to the current row. These are also window functions.

The following example searches for the previous start date and the next start date for each row. The offset is 1 in both cases.

```
SELECT empno, lname, fname, start_date,
    LAG(start_date, 1) OVER(ORDER BY start_date)
              AS previous_start_date,
    LEAD(start_date, 1) OVER(ORDER BY start_date)
              AS next_start_date
FROM employee
```

| empno | lname  | fname  | start_date | previous_start_date | next_start_date |
|-------|--------|--------|------------|---------------------|-----------------|
| 3547  | River  | Lilian | 2009-05-12 | NULL                | 2009-05-12      |
| 2884  | Taylor | Peter  | 2009-05-12 | 2009-05-12          | 2009-10-15      |
| 2234  | Wood   | Mike   | 2009-10-15 | 2009-05-12          | 2014-09-24      |
| 2245  | Brooke | Rachel | 2014-09-24 | 2009-10-15          | 2017-09-15      |
| 3546  | Brown  | Laura  | 2017-09-15 | 2014-09-24          | 2018-01-01      |
| 2345  | Lake   | Leon   | 2018-01-01 | 2017-09-15          | 2020-03-02      |
| 2134  | Stream | Peter  | 2020-03-02 | 2018-01-01          | NULL            |

## 20.8 Conditions to Formulate the Result Set

*Get projno, project_name, and priority. If priority is missing (NULL), fetch the average of all priorities.*

The upper query gives all rows where priority is not NULL. The second query searches for rows with NULL priority and calculates their average.

```
SELECT projno, project_name, priority , 'original' AS type
FROM project
WHERE priority IS NOT NULL
    UNION ALL
SELECT p1.projno, p1.project_name, AVG(p2.priority), 'avg'
FROM project p1
CROSS JOIN project p2          -- cartesian join
WHERE p1.priority IS NULL
GROUP BY p1.projno, p1.project_name
```

| projno | project_name | priority | type |
| ------ | ------------ | -------- | ------- |
| P1 | BOOKKEEPING | 2 | original |
| P2 | BILLING | 1 | original |
| P3 | WAREHOUSING | 3 | original |
| P4 | ACCOUNTING | 2 | original |
| P5 | CUSTOMERS | 3 | original |
| P6 | STATISTICS | 2 | avg |

This is kind of a conditional query, "If priority is NULL, then…".

We can get the same result also with a cross join, CASE, and COALESCE.

```
SELECT p.projno, p.project_name,
     COALESCE (p.priority, avg_query.average) AS priority,
      CASE
         WHEN p.priority IS NULL THEN 'avg'
         ELSE 'original'
      END AS type
FROM project p CROSS JOIN           -- average clued to each row
    (SELECT AVG(p1.priority) AS average
     FROM project p1) avg_query
```

## 20.9 Detail and Sum on the Same Row

Sometimes, we need to include both group-level and table-level sums on the same row in a SELECT statement. We might want to know the employee salary and its share of the total salary by city.

Here, we can use the "SELECT as a table" construct to calculate the total salaries by city and join that data to the employee table. Now we have both the individual employee salary and the department total salary on the same row:

*For each employee, fetch the salary and its percentage of the total department salary. Order by employee's last name.*

```
SELECT e.lname,
    ROUND(e.salary*100/dep_sum.dep_tot, 2) AS perc,
      e.salary, e.deptno, dep_sum.dep_tot
FROM employee e           -- in SQL Server use CAST to round
JOIN
  (SELECT deptno, SUM(salary) AS dep_tot
   FROM employee
   GROUP BY deptno) dep_sum
  ON COALESCE(e.deptno, -10) = COALESCE(dep_sum.deptno, -10)
ORDER BY e.lname
```

| lname | perc | salary | deptno | dep_tot |
|--------|--------|---------|--------|---------|
| Brooke | 100.00 | 3100.00 | 4 | 3100.00 |
| Brown | 46.09 | 2650.00 | 1 | 5750.00 |
| Lake | 33.33 | 2800.00 | 3 | 8400.00 |
| River | 33.33 | 2800.00 | 3 | 8400.00 |
| Stream | 33.33 | 2800.00 | 3 | 8400.00 |
| Taylor | 100.00 | 2960.00 | NULL | 2960.00 |
| Wood | 53.91 | 3100.00 | 1 | 5750.00 |

The formula for the percentage share is e.salary*100/dep_sum.dep_tot. The ROUND function will round and truncate to two decimals. In SQL Server, use CAST and convert to

DECIMAL (7, 2). One NULL is not equal to another NULL, so we use the COALESCE function, which converts NULL to -10.

An alternate solution using a self-join:

```
SELECT e1.lname,
    ROUND(e1.salary*100/SUM(e2.salary), 2) AS perc,
    e1.salary, e2.deptno, SUM(e2.salary) AS dep_tot
FROM employee e1
JOIN employee e2
 ON COALESCE(e1.deptno, -10) = COALESCE(e2.deptno, -10)
GROUP BY e1.lname,e1.salary, e2.deptno
ORDER BY e1.lname
```

Maybe the best way is to use the Window function Partition:

```
SELECT lname,
 ROUND(salary*100/(SUM(salary) OVER (PARTITION BY deptno)), 2)
      AS perc, salary, deptno,
      SUM(salary) OVER (PARTITION BY deptno) AS dep_tot
FROM employee
ORDER BY lname
```

In SQL Server, the ROUND function rounds but does not cut. Instead, use CAST and convert to DECIMAL (5,2).

**EXERCISES**

1.  Fetch the lname, fname, city, salary, and the salary's share of the city total salary together with city total salary. Order by lname. Use a subquery to get the city totals and use the subquery in the FROM clause:

```
SELECT ....
FROM  table
JOIN
(SELECT ...
   FROM table...) tab..
```

---

## 20.10 Grand Total and Subtotals

The SQL standard has features that are meant specifically for data warehouse use and reporting. Special grouping functions are an example.

Let´s first look at an example where we fetch hours by location and project for projects with employees (no outer join this time).

```
SELECT p.location, p.project_name, SUM(pe.hours_act) AS sum
FROM project p
     JOIN proj_emp pe
     ON p.projno = pe.projno
GROUP BY p.location, p.project_name
ORDER BY p.location, p.project_name

location        project_name        sum
--------        ------------        -----
HELSINKI        BILLING             700
HELSINKI        WAREHOUSING         900
LONDON          ACCOUNTING          900
LONDON          BOOKKEEPING         1600
```

Using GROUPING SETS, we can compute multiple GROUP BY clauses in one SQL statement. We group by location and project name together and also by location and project name separately. GROUPING SETS is not supported in MySQL. Instead, use the format "GROUP WITH ROLLUP" described below.

```
SELECT p.location, p.project_name, SUM(pe.hours_act) AS sum
FROM project p
    JOIN proj_emp pe
    ON p.projno = pe.projno
GROUP BY GROUPING SETS ((p.location, p.project_name),
        p.location, p.project_name)
ORDER BY p.location, p.project_name
```

```
location        project_name        sum
--------        ------------        ----
NULL            ACCOUNTING          900
NULL            BILLING             700
NULL            BOOKKEEPING         1600
NULL            WAREHOUSING         900
HELSINKI        NULL                1600
HELSINKI        BILLING             700
HELSINKI        WAREHOUSING         900
LONDON          NULL                2500
LONDON          ACCOUNTING          900
LONDON          BOOKKEEPING         1600
```

First, we see the grouping by project name, then by location, and finally by both location and project name.

Then, we test the ROLLUP keyword in the GROUP BY clause. It adds subtotal rows to the result set. ROLLUP sums from the lowest level upwards (the opposite of drilling down).

The next statement retrieves actual hours by location and project so that there are also subtotals when location changes and grand total.

```
SELECT p.location, p.project_name, SUM(pe.hours_act) AS sum
FROM project p
   JOIN proj_emp pe
   ON p.projno = pe.projno
GROUP BY ROLLUP (p.location, p.project_name)
```

| location | project_name | sum |
|----------|--------------|------|
| -------- | ------------ | ---- |
| HELSINKI | BILLING | 700 |
| HELSINKI | WAREHOUSING | 900 |
| HELSINKI | NULL | 1600 |
| LONDON | ACCOUNTING | 900 |
| LONDON | BOOKKEEPING | 1600 |
| LONDON | NULL | 2500 |
| NULL | NULL | 4100 |

Then, we introduce CUBE, which is a sort of an extension to ROLLUP (CUBE is not supported in MySQL).

```
SELECT p.location, p.project_name, SUM(pe.hours_act) AS sum
FROM project p
   JOIN proj_emp pe
   ON p.projno = pe.projno
GROUP BY CUBE (p.location , p.project_name)
```

| Location | project_name | sum |
|----------|--------------|------|
| -------- | ------------ | ---- |
| LONDON | ACCOUNTING | 900 |
| NULL | ACCOUNTING | 900 |
| HELSINKI | BILLING | 700 |
| NULL | BILLING | 700 |
| LONDON | BOOKKEEPING | 1600 |
| NULL | BOOKKEEPING | 1600 |
| HELSINKI | WAREHOUSING | 900 |
| NULL | WAREHOUSING | 900 |
| NULL | NULL | 4100 |
| HELSINKI | NULL | 1600 |
| LONDON | NULL | 2500 |

It groups the result set by all possible combinations and a grand total row, too. The order of rows may differ in your product. In the result set, NULL means "total". Row NULL NULL 4100 means Grand total 4100.

It is possible to make the result set a bit easier to read by using the GROUPING function:

```
SELECT p.location, p.project_name, SUM(pe.hours_act) AS sum,
   GROUPING(p.location) AS location_total,
   GROUPING(p.project_name) AS project_name_total
FROM project p
      JOIN proj_emp pe
      ON p.projno = pe.projno
GROUP BY CUBE (p.location , p.project_name)
```

| location | project_name | sum | location_total | project_name_total |
|----------|--------------|-----|----------------|--------------------|
| LONDON | ACCOUNTING | 900 | 0 | 0 |
| NULL | ACCOUNTING | 900 | 1 | 0 |
| HELSINKI | BILLING | 700 | 0 | 0 |
| NULL | BILLING | 700 | 1 | 0 |
| LONDON | BOOKKEEPING | 1600 | 0 | 0 |
| NULL | BOOKKEEPING | 1600 | 1 | 0 |
| HELSINKI | WAREHOUSING | 900 | 0 | 0 |
| NULL | WAREHOUSING | 900 | 1 | 0 |
| NULL | NULL | 4100 | 1 | 1 |
| HELSINKI | NULL | 1600 | 0 | 1 |
| LONDON | NULL | 2500 | 0 | 1 |

So the value of the GROUPING function is 1 if the row has the sum of the column. In "ordinary" rows, the value is 0.

We can add a bit more clarity by using CASE:

```
SELECT
CASE
    WHEN GROUPING (p.location) = 1 THEN 'TOTAL'
    ELSE COALESCE (p.location,'UNKNOWN')
END AS location,
CASE
    WHEN GROUPING (p.project_name) = 1 THEN 'TOTAL'
    ELSE COALESCE (p.project_name,'UNKNOWN')
END AS project_name,
SUM(pe.hours_act) AS sum
FROM project p
    JOIN proj_emp pe
    ON p.projno = pe.projno
GROUP BY CUBE (p.location , p.project_name)
```

| location | project_name | sum |
| -------- | ---------------- | ----- |
| LONDON | ACCOUNTING | 900 |
| TOTAL | ACCOUNTING | 900 |
| HELSINKI | BILLING | 700 |
| TOTAL | BILLING | 700 |
| LONDON | BOOKKEEPING | 1600 |
| TOTAL | BOOKKEEPING | 1600 |
| HELSINKI | WAREHOUSING | 900 |
| TOTAL | WAREHOUSING | 900 |
| TOTAL | TOTAL | 4100 |
| HELSINKI | TOTAL | 1600 |
| LONDON | TOTAL | 2500 |

One more example using COALESCE. We fetch sum of salary and count of employees for each city, and grand total row too.

```
SELECT COALESCE (city, '**TOTAL') AS city,
         SUM(salary) AS total_salary,
         COUNT(*) AS count
FROM employee
GROUP BY ROLLUP(city)
ORDER BY  total_salary
```

```
city      total_salary      count
--------  ------------      ------
SYDNEY    5450.00           2
HELSINKI  6060.00           2
LONDON    8700.00           3
**TOTAL   20210.00          7
```

Note that ROLLUP is always connected to the GROUP BY clause. You cannot use it for "ordinary" totals. Here is an example of this:

```
SELECT empno, lname, salary,
         'ROW' AS type  -- "type" to make total come last
FROM employee
UNION
SELECT 'TOTAL ', '                ', SUM(salary) , 'TOTAL'
FROM employee
ORDER BY 4, 2
```

```
empno    lname      salary      type
------   ---------  -------     -----
2245     Brooke     3100.00     ROW
3546     Brown      2650.00     ROW
2345     Lake       2800.00     ROW
3547     River      2800.00     ROW
2134     Stream     2800.00     ROW
2884     Taylor     2960.00     ROW
2234     Wood       3100.00     ROW
TOTAL               20210.00    TOTAL
```

## 20.11 Crosstab Query

Many are used to do crosstab operations (PivotTable) in Excel. The goal is to turn columns into rows, or vice versa. SQL has a special statement for that, PIVOT. But let's first look at a traditional crosstab formulation using CASE.

Column headers are normally taken from the table definition and are not data but metadata. For crosstab, we need data from rows to column headers. First, we introduce a method that works on all of our databases.

*Retrieve actual hours for all employees by project in a crosstab format.*

```
SELECT empno,
  SUM(CASE projno WHEN 'P1' THEN hours_act ELSE 0 END) AS P1,
  SUM(CASE projno WHEN 'P2' THEN hours_act ELSE 0 END) AS P2,
  SUM(CASE projno WHEN 'P3' THEN hours_act ELSE 0 END) AS P3,
  SUM(CASE projno WHEN 'P4' THEN hours_act ELSE 0 END) AS P4
FROM proj_emp
GROUP BY empno
ORDER BY empno
```

| EMPNO | P1 | P2 | P3 | P4 |
|------|-----|-----|-----|-----|
| 2134 | 300 | 300 | 0 | 0 |
| 2234 | 200 | 0 | 0 | 300 |
| 2245 | 200 | 400 | 900 | 200 |
| 2345 | 100 | 0 | 0 | 0 |
| 2884 | 100 | 0 | 0 | 400 |
| 3546 | 400 | 0 | 0 | 0 |
| 3547 | 300 | 0 | 0 | 0 |

Note that the column headers are as if hardcoded into place using the AS word. In fact, there is no actual summation, but the SUM function is needed to get the grouping to work.

Oracle, Snowflake, and SQL Server support the PIVOT operator.

Oracle and Snowflake:

```
SELECT *
FROM
    (SELECT empno, projno, hours_act
      FROM proj_emp) k
PIVOT
 (
 SUM(hours_act)   FOR projno
 IN ('P1', 'P2', 'P3', 'P4')
 )   p
ORDER BY empno
```

SQL Server:

```
SELECT *                     -- or SELECT empno, P1, P2, P3, P4
FROM
    (SELECT empno, projno, hours_act
      FROM proj_emp) k
PIVOT
 (SUM(hours_act)   FOR projno
 IN (P1, P2, P3, P4)        -- or square brackets (e.g. [P1])
 ) AS p
ORDER BY empno
```

Pivot has three parts: row identifiers, column identifiers, and aggregates. Above, empno is the row identifier, column identifier is projno, and aggregate is the sum of hours_act.

PostgreSQL has a proprietary CROSSTAB function instead of PIVOT. MySQL, DB2, and Hive do not have a PIVOT function. Use the CASE method described above in these products.

UNPIVOT turns columns into rows. You can use it in SQL Server, Snowflake, and Oracle. Example:

```
SELECT empno, empcol, value
FROM
    (SELECT empno, fname, lname, city
     FROM employee) emp
UNPIVOT
    (value FOR empcol IN
        (fname, lname, city)
     ) AS u
ORDER BY 1, 2
```

```
empno     empcol        value
-------   ---------     -------
2134      city          LONDON
2134      fname         Peter
2134      lname         Stream
2234      city          LONDON
2234      fname         Mike
2234      lname         Wood
2245      city          HELSINKI
2245      fname         Rachel
2245      lname         Brooke
2345      city          LONDON
2345      fname         Leon
2345      lname         Lake
etc.
```

MySQL, DB2, Hive, and PostgreSQL do not include UNPIVOT. This query will give you the same result:

```
SELECT empno, 'fname' AS empcol, fname AS value FROM employee
UNION ALL
SELECT empno, 'lname', lname FROM employee
UNION ALL
SELECT empno, 'city', city FROM employee
ORDER BY 1, 2
```

Column headers come from the first SELECT.

## 20.12 Formulation of Column Alias Name

You can formulate column alias names by adding blanks, dots, commas, or other punctuation marks. Or start the column name with a number or even have a number as the column name. In these cases, you must put the alias name in double quotes ("), otherwise you get an error message.

Example:

```
SELECT empno AS "employee number",     -- contains a space
       education AS "educ.",           -- dot in name
       city AS "2city",                -- starts with number
       deptno AS "123"                 -- alias is a number
FROM employee

employee number      educ.   2city        123
---------------      -------  ----------   -----------
2134                 Ba      LONDON       3
2234                 PhD     LONDON       1
2245                 MA      HELSINKI     4
2345                 NULL    LONDON       3
2884                 MA      HELSINKI     NULL
3546                 Ba      SYDNEY       1
3547                 DIP     SYDNEY       3
```

In SQL Server, you can also use brackets ([]).

# CHAPTER TWENTY ONE

# Updating

## 21.1 Updating Data from Another Table

Often, we want to update a table using data from another table. This can be done in a single query.

*The table 'empchange' has the changed salary and tax rate of some of our employees. Update the new values in the employee table.*

Here are the contents of the empchange table:

```
EMPNO     SALARY    TAX_RATE
----  ----------  ----------
2345        2900        25.5
3546        2750          23
```

The following works in all products in this book except Snowflake and MySQL (see solutions for them below):

```
UPDATE employee e
SET (salary, tax_rate) =
    (SELECT ec.salary, ec.tax_rate
     FROM empchange ec
     WHERE e.empno = ec.empno)
WHERE e.empno IN
      (SELECT empno
       FROM empchange)
```

The subquery in the SET clause provides the changed values for the employee table. With the help of the last subquery, the changes only affect employees that have changed. Without the WHERE clause, the salary and tax rate for employees not in the empchange table would be set to NULL.

After the update, two rows have been changed:

| EMPNO | FNAME | LNAME | SALARY | TAX_RATE |
|-------|-------|-------|--------|----------|
| 2134 | Peter | Stream | 2800 | 22 |
| 2234 | Mike | Wood | 3100 | 33 |
| 2245 | Rachel | Brooke | 3100 | 31 |
| 2345 | Leon | Lake | 2900 | 25.5 |
| 2884 | Peter | Taylor | 2960 | 31 |
| 3546 | Laura | Brown | 2750 | 23 |
| 3547 | Lilian | River | 2800 | 37 |

MySQL has a handy extension where the UPDATE can be part of a join:

```
UPDATE employee e
JOIN empchange ec
   ON e.empno = ec.empno
SET e.salary = ec.salary,
    e.tax_rate = ec.tax_rate
```

SQL Server also has a join-based solution:

```
UPDATE e
SET e.salary = ec.salary,
    e.tax_rate = ec.tax_rate
FROM employee e JOIN empchange ec
      ON e.empno = ec.empno
```

In Snowflake, you can use this similar construction:

```
UPDATE employee e
SET e.salary = ec.salary,
    e.tax_rate = ec.tax_rate
FROM   empchange ec
    WHERE e.empno = ec.empno
```

## 21.2 Insert and Update at the Same Time

Sometimes, we might want to update a table with information from another table so that if the row already exists, it is updated with the new data, and if it is missing, a new row is inserted. The SQL 2003 standard defined the handy statement MERGE (i.e., "UPSERT"), with which you can insert and update at the same time.

We have a table with updates to the project table, called changedata. The priority of P1 has changed and then there are two new projects:

```
PROJNO PROJECT_NAME        PRIORITY LOCATION
------ --------------- ---------- ---------------
P1     BOOKKEEPING            1 LONDON
P13    PURCHASING             3 HELSINKI
P14    HR                     2 LONDON
```

The following statement updates the existing rows (1 row) and adds the missing ones (2 rows):

```
MERGE INTO project p
USING
     (SELECT projno, project_name, priority, location
        FROM changedata) c
  ON (p.projno = c.projno)
WHEN MATCHED THEN                     -- matched ones are updated
   UPDATE SET p.priority = c.priority
WHEN NOT MATCHED THEN                 -- non-matched are added
   INSERT (projno, project_name, priority, location)
   VALUES (c.projno, c.project_name, c.priority, c.location)
```

The project table now looks like this:

```
PROJNO  PROJECT_NAME      PRIORITY    LOCATION
------  ----------------  ----------  ----------------
P1      BOOKKEEPING              1    LONDON
P2      BILLING                 1    HELSINKI
P3      WAREHOUSING             3    HELSINKI
P4      ACCOUNTING              2    LONDON
P5      CUSTOMERS               3    SINGAPORE
P6      STATISTICS           NULL    NULL
P14     HR                      2    LONDON
P13     PURCHASING              3    HELSINKI
```

---

## 21.3 Generating New Rows from the Same Table

You can generate new rows in the same table using the existing rows. Here, we add a new project to the project table, similar to P2 but with the name P2a and with a priority of 2.

```
INSERT INTO project (projno, project_name, priority, location)
SELECT 'P2a', project_name, 2, location
FROM project
WHERE projno = 'P2'
```

Let's take a look at the new contents of the project table:

```
SELECT *
FROM project

PROJNO PROJECT_NAME    PRIORITY   LOCATION
------ --------------- ---------- ---------------
P1     BOOKKEEPING            2 LONDON
P2     BILLING               1 HELSINKI
P3     WAREHOUSING           3 HELSINKI
P4     ACCOUNTING            2 LONDON
P5     CUSTOMERS             3 SINGAPORE
P6     STATISTICS         NULL NULL
P2a    BILLING               2 HELSINKI
```

Naturally, the two tables can be different ones.

## 21.4 Swapping Column Data

Let's assume the project_name and location columns switched places during table loading. The following statement will swap them.

```
UPDATE project
SET project_name = location,
location = project_name
```

Please note that the following is **not** equivalent:

```
UPDATE project
SET project_name = location;
UPDATE project
SET location = project_name;
```

---

## 21.5 Updating a Column with a Value Dependent on a Value in Other Column

The CASE function can be used to conditionally update a column depending on the value of another column on the same row. You can run your update in a single statement instead of two or more statements.

*Update the priority for the London projects to 6 and Helsinki projects to 9.*

```
UPDATE project
SET priority =
    CASE location
            WHEN 'LONDON' THEN 6
            WHEN 'HELSINKI' THEN 9
            ELSE priority        -- otherwise stays the same
        END
```

# CHAPTER TWENTY TWO

# Performance Considerations

We will first cover the basics of the optimizer and the optimizer's explain plans. It is important to understand the effect of indexes. Note that there are no indexes in Snowflake. It has other efficient methods for performance. Finally, we provide a list of potentially slow query formats. Some modern databases, such as Oracle and SQL Server, have features that can automatically generate indexes. In any case, it is very useful to understand the underlying principles.

## 22.1 SQL and Performance

The performance of a SQL statement depends on several factors. One important factor is how the database is designed and what kind of indexes are defined. In companies, the definition of indexes usually belongs to the tasks of database administrators and requires expertise in that area. On the other hand, it is good for the SQL programmer to know how to study the explain plans of his or her own commands, which, with a little interpretation, shows how good performance can be expected.

It is also good to measure the execution time of the instructions. It is possible to equip the SQL statements with a hint that guides the optimizer in critical situations.

## 22.2 The Optimizer

The optimizer of database management systems is an internal program that accepts a SQL command and produces alternative physical search methods for it. It then tries to choose the most efficient one. That is, the one that performs the least disk operations, consumes the least amount of processor time, and causes as few sorts as possible.

We already talked about indexes in the Index chapter. The index is like the index at the end of this book. It is in alphabetical or numerical order and each entry has a direct reference (page number) to the right place. If you want to know everything about "CASE", you could read every page and row, and surely you will find every instance of CASE. Another method is to search the index for the word "CASE" and then do several direct searches to the correct pages.

Let's look at a simple example of data. The task is to retrieve people named "Brown" from the person table and get the columns person_id, last_name, and pin_code. We assume that there are one million people in the person table. There are 0.05 percent (500) of people named Brown. An index has been created for the column last_name.

Here is the query:

```
SELECT  person_id, last_name, pin_code
FROM person
WHERE last_name = 'Brown'
```

The optimizer has two options to perform this logical level ("what") query at the physical level ("how"):

- **Full table scan**. Read the table from the beginning to find rows with name Brown. This is called a full table scan. This requires scanning the entire table because "Brown" might appear in the last row. The search time was approx. 6-7 seconds in the test.

- **Index-based search**. Search for rows containing "Brown" from the index. With the pointers obtained for each row containing "Brown", the corresponding rows in the table can be directly accessed (resulting in 500 hash operations in the table). The search time in the test was approximately one second.

The first option causes more disk operations and takes more time because the table is not small, and only a small number of entries have the name Brown. In the second option, the database quickly locates "Brown" entries in the index since they are adjacent and performs about 500 scattered disk reads to access the relevant rows in the table (as individuals named "Brown" are likely dispersed throughout the table). Therefore, option 2 is faster. As the table size increases, the advantage of the index will grow.

The optimizer uses many inputs to support its decision making. It needs to know about existing indexes, the number of rows in each table, and the distribution of values. If the last_name column had no index, the optimizer would have ended up with a full table scan. If only a thousand people were in the person table, the optimizer would not use the index because table scan is already faster. If there were 5% of Brown names in a million rows of data, a good optimizer would also end up with a table scan because there would be a Brown on almost every database page.

## The Execution Plan

We can ask the optimizer to tell what kind of execution plan it is planning to use. In the terminology, we ask the optimizer to explain the plan.

The content of the execution plan differs slightly in products, but the main points are:

1. The steps needed to run the query.
2. Use of indexes. The execution plan tells which indexes are used.
3. Table scan. The table is scanned without an index.

4. Join method and order of tables in join, e.g., nested loops, hash join, and sort-merge join.

5. Sorting.

6. Cost. A relative estimate of the performance load.

In most products, there is a handy way in the query interface to get the execution plan for a given query. A few examples of execution plans will be introduced shortly.

In Oracle SQL Developer, you can request the execution plan by pressing F10 or the Explain plan icon. Or add one of the following rows just before the SELECT.

```
EXPLAIN PLAN FOR        or      SET AUTOTRACE ON
SELECT...                        SELECT...
```

In SQL Server Management Studio, press the button Display Estimated Execution plan.

In MySQL, Snowflake, Hive, and PostgreSQL, put the word EXPLAIN before the SELECT.

---

## 22.3 Multicolumn Indexes

A multicolumn index has been created for the columns projno and empno in the table proj_emo. The index was created like this:

```
CREATE INDEX pe_projno_empno ON proj_emp(projno, empno)
```

Look at the following figure. While the rows in the table are in random order, projno and empno are in order in the index. The rows in the index have a reference (RID: RowId) to the corresponding table row. The index leafpage shown in the figure has its own tree index for fast searching (not in the picture).

**Index pe_projno_empno**

| projno | empno | rid |
|--------|-------|------|
| P1 | 2134 | RID.. |
| P1 | 2234 | RID.. |
| P1 | 2245 | RID.. |
| P1 | 2345 | RID.. |
| P1 | 2884 | RID.. |
| P1 | 3546 | RID.. |
| P1 | 3547 | RID.. |
| P2 | 2134 | RID.. |
| P2 | 2245 | 400 |
| P3 | 2245 | 900 |
| ... | ... | ... |

**Table proj_emp**

| projno | empno | hours_act | hour_est |
|--------|-------|-----------|----------|
| P2 | 2134 | 300 | NULL |
| P1 | 2134 | 300 | 300 |
| P4 | 2234 | 300 | 400 |
| P3 | 2245 | 900 | 100 |
| P1 | 2234 | 200 | NULL |
| P1 | 2245 | 200 | 300 |
| ... | ... | ... | ... |

Figure 21: The pro_emp table, whose columns projno and empno have a multicolumn index. Pointers in the rid column of the index refer directly to the rows of the table. Only a part of rows and pointers are shown in the picture.

Note that this is a non-clustered index. The rows in the table are also ordered in a clustered index, according to the index. Clustered indexes are often better in terms of performance. SQL Server, MySQL (InnoDB), and DB2 support clustered indexes.

The next two WHERE statements lead to the use of an index-based table search, because in the index, the values are found quickly and in the right order.

```
1) WHERE projno = 'P2'    -- Seach using the whole index
   AND empno = '2245'
2) WHERE projno = 'P2'    -- Search using the first part of the
                          --  index
```

In the following case, the optimizer does not use an index (not in order) but ends up in a table scan.

```
WHERE empno = '2245'    -- Search trying to use the last part
                        --  of the index
```

This is like trying to find a first name from a telephone catalog, which is sorted by last name and first name order.

## Superfast Queries using Covering Indexes

In this section, we examine how indexes affect the optimizer's decisions when choosing an access path search path. In addition, we show the optimizer's execution plans for the queries. The execution plan examples are from Oracle. Similar reports are available in other products, too. Let's look at the following query:

```
SELECT lname, fname
FROM employee
WHERE city = 'SYDNEY'
AND deptno = 3
```

Here is the execution plan for the query above:

```
--------------------------------------------------------------------
| Id  | Operation          | Name     | Rows  | Bytes | Cost (%CPU)| Time     |
--------------------------------------------------------------------
|   0 | SELECT STATEMENT   |          |     1 |    34 |     3  (0)| 00:00:01 |
|*  1 |  TABLE ACCESS FULL | EMPLOYEE |     1 |    34 |     3  (0)| 00:00:01 |
--------------------------------------------------------------------
```

The optimizer does a full table scan to find all records from Sydney with deptno 3. This can be slow if the table is large. To speed up the query, a good index would be a multicolumn index:

```
CREATE INDEX emp_2 ON employee (city, deptno)
```

Then, we execute the exact same query:

```
SELECT lname, fname
FROM employee
WHERE city = 'SYDNEY'
AND deptno = 3
```

Execution plan:

```
--------------------------------------------------------------------
|   0 | SELECT STATEMENT                         |          |  1 |  34 |  2 (0)| 00:00:01 |
|   1 |  TABLE ACCESS BY INDEX ROWID BATCHED| EMPLOYEE |  1 |  34 |  2 (0)| 00:00:01 |
|*  2 |   INDEX RANGE SCAN                       | EMP_2    |  1 |     |  1 (0)| 00:00:01 |
--------------------------------------------------------------------
```

Now the execution plan shows that the index emp_2 is used first, then table access. Read from bottom to top. But you can build a **superfast query** by using a **covering index**. We include the columns we are actually retrieving (the SELECT list) at the end of the index.

```
CREATE INDEX emp_3 ON employee (city, deptno, lname, fname)
```

This index allows for the most efficient query possible: the entire **search is done directly from the index** without having to go to the table at all. Such a multipart index is called a covering index. The query execution plan report below shows that only the index is touched (the table name is not mentioned). This minimizes disk operations because the index is in order and all rows needed are close together. Slow random reads to the table are not needed.

We run the same query once more, without modifications:

```
SELECT lname, fname
FROM employee
WHERE city = 'SYDNEY'
AND deptno = 3
```

Execution plan:

```
-----------------------------------------------------------------------
| Id  | Operation          | Name  | Rows  | Bytes | Cost (%CPU)| Time     |
-----------------------------------------------------------------------
|   0 | SELECT STATEMENT   |       |     1 |    34 |     1  (0)| 00:00:01 |
|*  1 |   INDEX RANGE SCAN| EMP_3 |     1 |    34 |     1  (0)| 00:00:01 |
-----------------------------------------------------------------------
```

Now we see that only the index emp_3 is accessed.

Of course, if the columns in the covering index are volatile, meaning that they change often, the updates might get a bit slower. Still, names change relatively rarely, and the update might get only two times slower (say, from 0.2 to 0.4 seconds). But the query above might get 20 or more times faster with that covering index!

There are cases where a whole application has been tuned much faster by first checking the most common SQL statements and then adding good covering indexes to support them.

This compound effect speeds up the whole application, without touching the application code! Also, in the data warehouse environment, you can tune reporting queries and ETL - processes this way.

A more difficult task for the optimizer than the previous one is to decide the correct order in join operations. Often, the tables are of very different sizes, and knowing how to join the tables in the right order significantly impacts performance. The optimizer has a lot to think about here because while three tables can be joined in six different orders, there are already a huge number of options when connecting five tables!

### Table Scan Benefits

Sometimes, a full table scan is better than using indexes. If you are looking for some value that is very common, using an index does not help. It is faster to read pages from the database in sequence than to look from index and then table, again index and then table, etc. If the rows you are searching for form a certain percent, the optimizer chooses table scan instead of indexed access. This percent can be as low as 5 percent.

---

## 22.4 Examples of Slow SQL Statements

Some SELECT structures might be slow. They produce the right result set, but the optimizer chooses a slow access path. Often, an index is not used even when there is a good index. Many slow queries can be rewritten to be faster.

The examples below are from our familiar training database. The tables are so small that all queries are fast. Imagine that the tables would include millions of rows.

Don´t include extra tables in your join (tables that are not necessary).

Avoid unnecessary columns in the SELECT list.

A function can prevent the use of an index. In the example below, an index was created for column city.

```
SELECT   empno, lname, fname
FROM employee
WHERE SUBSTRING(city, 1, 1) = 'L'    -- Oracle, DB2: use SUBSTR
```

The execution plan tells that the access path is a full table scan. The index is not used.

In the following query, the optimizer chooses to do an index scan.

```
SELECT   empno, lname, fname
FROM employee
WHERE city LIKE 'L%'
```

Avoid, if possible, a LIKE as in the following query. The optimizer cannot use an index.

```
WHERE city LIKE '%ond%'
```

Negation:

```
SELECT   empno, lname, fname
FROM employee
WHERE city <> 'LONDON'
```

In many products, the optimizer tends not to use the index for negation queries. This is probably a good thing because most of the table is being searched (the non-Londoners are likely to be the majority), so the table scan is faster than using the index.

Calculation in the WHERE clause:

```
SELECT   empno, lname, fname
FROM employee
WHERE salary + 100 = 3200
```

The index for column salary is not used. Use the following format:

```
SELECT   empno, lname, fname
FROM employee
WHERE salary = 3100
```

Avoid using the NOT IN subquery, as it is potentially slow. Use NOT EXISTS or LEFT JOIN with NULL check instead (see Chapter 10.2). Although optimizers, in many cases, can internally convert a subquery into a join before execution.

UNION ALL is faster, so use it instead of UNION if the SELECT queries are not producing duplicates.

Don't use DISTINCT unless you really need to remove duplicate rows from the result set. The removal of duplicate rows is often done by sorting, which might be slow. Also, keep this slowness in mind when using ORDER BY for large row sets.

Let´s look at this join:

```
SELECT d.deptno, d.deptname,
        e.lname, e.fname, e.city
  FROM department d
      JOIN employee e
        ON (d.deptno = e.deptno)
  WHERE e.city = 'LONDON'
  ORDER BY d.deptname
```

The deptno in employee table is the primary key, so it is indexed. If deptno in department table is not indexed, the query might be slow. Always index foreign key columns to speed up joins.

# Index